Publisher: Military History Group, London, United Kingdom.
E-Mail: milhisgroup@gmail.com
Print: Lulu Press, Inc., Lulu Press, Inc. 627 Davis Drive Suite 300 Morrisville, NC 27560, USA. Massachusetts, US; Wisconsin, US; Ontario, Canada; Île-de-France, France; Wielkopolska, Poland; Cambridgeshire, United Kingdom; Victoria, Australia.

ISBN 978-1-915453-10-5

IS-2
Development, Design & Production
of Stalin's Warhammer

Peter Samsonov

Military History Group

Table of Contents

Acknowledgements

The author would like to thank Yuri Pasholok for providing a considerable amount of documents that made this book possible. The author would also like to thank Pavel Borovikov and Nikita Trutnev for photographs provided for the use of this book as well as the Patriot Park museum, Kubinka tank museum, Canadian War Museum, and Imperial War Museum Duxford, whose exhibits serve as illustrations in this book.

In Search of a Heavy Tank 1919-1942

The First "Heavy" Tanks

The first heavy tanks (or at least what was considered a heavy tank at the time) on Russian soil were foreign built. Without a sophisticated industry capable of producing anything heavier than armored cars, the Russian Imperial Army had to rely on foreign aid to get a taste of this weapon. Their chance came not during the First World War, but only afterwards, during the Russian Civil War. 12 British tanks arrived in Novorossiysk on April 13th, 1919, as war aid for the White Army.[1] This shipment and those that followed included both the Mark V heavy tanks and Whippet medium tanks.[2] These tanks eventually ended up in the hands of the Red Army, whether during the war or after its conclusion.[3] The tanks were accepted into service under the name Ricardo (after the brand of the engine), but their design showed little long-term promise. Unlike the Renault FT, which inspired a copy named Russian Renault, the Mark V was an evolutionary dead end. These tanks alone could not make up the Red Army's heavy tank force, as by 1929 only 45 were operational.[4]

There were different ideas as to where to go from here. As Soviet industry began to mature to the point where an indigenous tank could be designed, several vehicle concepts arose. The first was the class of support vehicles. It consisted of two-man tanks armed with a machine

---

[1] Ye. Belash, *Tanki Mezhvoyennogo Perioda*, Tactical Press, Moscow, 2014. p.10
[2] RGVA F.4 Op.19 D.55 L.24-27
[3] M.R. Habeck, *Storm of Steel The Development of Armor Doctrine in Germany and the Soviet Union, 1919–1939*, Kindle Edition, p. 68.
[4] L. Samuelson, *Plans for Stalin's War Machine*, http://militera.lib.ru/research/samuelson_l/05.html, retrieved on October 4th, 2021

gun and a cannon[5] and "machinegunettes" (*pulemyotka*), small one-man vehicles armed with only a machine gun. The more familiar term "tankette" (*tanketka)* is also used to refer to these vehicles. As the name implies, the job of this class of armored vehicle was to directly support infantry and cavalry on the battlefield.[6]

The other class of vehicle defined by 1927 was the maneuver tank (*manevrenniy tank*). These tanks were much more versatile than the support tanks. This class of tank was meant to fight independently, capable of both breakthroughs[7] that later became associated with heavy tanks and long-range exploitation[8] action that was later associated with medium and light tanks, such as those from the BT series (*bystrokhodny tank*, fast tank).[9]

A "large tank" was also envisioned, but in a purely experimental form. Plans made in 1928 called for production of just two such vehicles in 1930-1931, compared to 665 small tanks, 300 medium tanks, and 290 tankettes.[10]

---

[5] Here and in subsequent occurrences the term "gun" refers to a high velocity weapon with a relatively high ratio of barrel length to caliber. "Howitzer" refers to a low velocity weapon with a relatively low ratio of barrel length to caliber, and "cannon" refers to either.
[6] M.N. Svirin, *Bronya Krepka: Istoriya sovetskogo tanka 1917-1939*, http://militera.lib.ru/tw/svirin_mn1/03.html, retrieved on August 21st, 2021
[7] A breakthrough action involves engaging enemy forces and breaking through their line of defense. These are typically short range actions.
[8] Breakthrough exploitation involves sending a lighter but faster moving force through an existing breakthrough in order to attack into the depth of enemy territory.
[9] M.N. Svirin, *Bronya Krepka: Istoriya sovetskogo tanka 1917-1939*, http://militera.lib.ru/tw/svirin_mn1/03.html, retrieved on August 21st, 2021
[10] L. Samuelson, *Plans for Stalin's War Machine*, http://militera.lib.ru/research/samuelson_l/05.html, retrieved on October 4th, 2021

4 Types of Tanks (1929)

To allow the maneuver tanks to fight independently, this type of tank needed more powerful armament, armor, and engine than the support tanks. The T-12 maneuver tank would have a high velocity 45 mm cannon (a 57 mm howitzer was also considered) and three machine guns. It would have a 180 hp engine and a top speed of 26 kph. 22 mm thick armor offered reliable protection from high caliber machine guns.[11] Weighing in at 15 tons, it was comparable with the British Medium Tank Mk.II designed around the mid-1920s.[12] The T-12's characteristics were far more impressive than those of the MS-1, which was armed with a 37 mm gun and a machine gun. Its 35 hp engine gave it a top speed of 15 kph.[13]

The vehicle classes were updated in July of 1929, at a meeting of the Revolutionary Military Council of the USSR (RVS: *Revolutsionniy Voyenniy Sovet*). The RVS defined four classes of vehicles. The convertible drive tankette was a small, light, and cheap vehicle intended for reconnaissance and rapid attacks where resistance was expected to be light. The small support tank was intended to fight alongside infantry in mechanized units, similar to what the British would later call an infantry tank. The maneuver (medium) tank was intended for fighting independently from infantry, either during breakthroughs or breakthrough exploitation action. Not much is said about the fourth class:

> "d) As for the large tank, limit ourselves to a theoretical development on this topic. Propose the Supreme Council of Economics Moscow Polytechnical Institute (MPU VSNKh) to

---

[11] A.G. Solyankin and others, *Sovetskiye sredniye tanki 1924-1941*, Tseyghaus, Moscow, 2007 p.4

[12] M.N. Svirin, *Bronya Krepka: Istoriya sovetskogo tanka 1917-1939*, http://militera.lib.ru/tw/svirin_mn1/03.html, retrieved on August 21st, 2021

[13] A.G. Solyankin and others, *Sovetskiye legkie tanki 1920-1941*, Tseyghaus, Moscow, 2007 p.14

present a draft project by October 1st, 1930, after which the issue of including it in the system of armament will be decided..."[14]

The "large tank" resurfaces again later that year, in a Politburo decree issued on December 5th, 1929. It seems that the MPU did not have much luck with this design.

"Aside from the T-18 tank, there are no designs for medium tanks, large tanks, or tankettes."[15]

The decree sets a production plan for 1930: 300 MS-1 small tanks, 30 T-12 maneuver (medium) tanks, and 10 tankettes.[16] Although the "large tank" concept is mentioned here again, it does not appear that any concrete work has been completed. Note that the production plans made in 1929 are smaller than the plans made in 1928. The number of small tanks was cut by more than half, medium tanks by tenfold, and tankettes were almost eliminated entirely. In addition to not having modern and competitive designs as noted in the Politburo decree, the constraints of the fledgling Soviet industry were being felt.

Habeck writes:

"Throughout 1929 plans for building an armor force and for its use in battle grew even more ambitious, far outstripping the ability of Soviet industry to produce the actual machines."[17]

Nevertheless, the army eagerly awaited its heavy tanks.

---

[14]   M.N.   Svirin,   *Bronya   Krepka: Istoriya   sovetskogo   tanka   1917-1939*, http://militera.lib.ru/tw/svirin_mn1/04.html, retrieved on August 21st, 2021
[15] RGASPI F.17 Op.162 D.8 L.18-19
[16] RGASPI F.17 Op.162 D.8 L.18-19
[17] M.R. Habeck, *Storm of Steel The Development of Armor Doctrine in Germany and the Soviet Union, 1919–1939*, Kindle Edition, p. 103.

"Taking no notice of these difficulties, the latest army mobilization plan, Variant #10, required twelve light tank battalions and one detached heavy tank battalion in the short term."[18]

It is difficult to say what these heavy tanks would be or how they would be used. The aforementioned Mark Vs were few in number, worn out, and obsolete. As for domestic designs, there was nothing at all to choose from.[19]

On December 13th, a note from Chief of the General Staff Shaposhnikov to Voroshilov described the types of foreign tanks that would be desirable for purchase. Among them is the "Vickers large tank", the 12-ton Vickers Mk.II.[20] However, the commission sent to look for heavy tanks abroad returned without success. A RVS meeting held on May 8th, 1931, established that while the foreign-bought Carden-Loyd tankette, Vickers 6-ton tank, and Christie fast tank were acceptable to fill the roles of the tankette, light tank, and fast tank destroyer respectively, no satisfactory heavy tank had been found.

The Directorate of Mechanization and Motorization (*Upravleniye Mechanizatsii i Motorizatsii*, UMM) was founded in 1929. Whereas the RVS was a high-level organization that provided high-level requirements, the UMM worked with design organizations. As such it was responsible for developing more concrete requirements and also dealt with acquiring tanks abroad, among other activities. Habeck notes about the UMM:

---

[18] M.R. Habeck, *Storm of Steel The Development of Armor Doctrine in Germany and the Soviet Union, 1919–1939*, Kindle Edition, p.103
[19] L. Samuelson, *Plans for Stalin's War Machine*, http://militera.lib.ru/research/samuelson_l/05.html, retrieved on October 4th, 2021
[20] RGVA F.31811 Op.1 D.38 L.2-3

"The regulations for the UMM envisioned a department that combined technical, production, supply, training, and, to a more limited extent, tactical functions."[21]

As such, the UMM was instructed to seek heavy tanks in the UK, Italy, and France with the goal of buying a sample or at least blueprints, although no specification of these potential heavy tanks is given.[22]

The Soviet government was cautious about heavy tank production. The plan for tank production composed on May 20th, 1930, by the Deputy Chief of the UMM Mobilization Department Lebed for 1929-1933 called for just 2 heavy tanks built in the 1930-1931 reporting year, compared to 665 small tanks, 300 medium tanks, and 290 tankettes. 200 heavy tanks were expected by 1933, compared to 2935 light tanks, 2430 medium tanks, and 1100 tankettes. A mobilization plan composed by the Red Army Staff by January 7th, 1930, had an even more pessimistic opinion of when these tanks would be available. The first 25 heavy tanks were awaited only in 1931-1932. After a discussion between the UMM and Red Army staff this number was slashed even further. No heavy tanks would be built in 1932, but 2512 small tanks, 736 medium tanks, and 755 tankettes were expected.[23]

Caution against heavier tanks can also be seen in other sources. For instance, notable military theorist Mikhail Nikolayevich Tukhachevskiy wrote to the head of the UMM Innokenty Andreevich Khalepsky on March 3rd, 1931. His letter described six different types of tanks, the heaviest of which was the "artillery destroyer tank" (*tank istrebitel artillerii*). This type of tank weighed up to 20 tons in order to meet weight limits of bridges. Tukhachevskiy presumed that this would be enough to give it sufficient front armor to withstand battalion level anti-tank

[21] M.R. Habeck, *Storm of Steel The Development of Armor Doctrine in Germany and the Soviet Union, 1919–1939*, Kindle Edition, p.113
[22] RGVA F.4 Op.14 D.414 L.20-22
[23] L. Samuelson, *Plans for Stalin's War Machine*, http://militera.lib.ru/research/samuelson_l/05.html, retrieved on October 4th, 2021

artillery and 75 mm HE shells from the front. The sides only needed to be thick enough to withstand fire from high caliber machine guns. It would still be fairly fast with a top speed of 30-40 kph.[24]

Even though the Red Army was still not certain what it wanted from a heavy tank, there was a consensus that such a tank was needed. Two proposals were made at a Supreme Council of Economics[25] subcommission meeting on January 6th, 1930, to prepare factories for heavy tank production (the term "heavy tank" rather than "large tank" began to enter common use in the early 1930s as tanks began to be defined by weight categories rather than the tank's purpose on the battlefield).[26] Counselor Postnikov proposed that production be set up at the Kramatorsk and Sverdlovsk heavy machinebuilding factories, while counselor Uryvayev suggested the Bolshevik and Barricade arms factories.[27]

Calls for Heavier Tanks (1929-1933)

While some thinkers opposed building tanks that were significantly heavier than those already in service, others were thinking bigger. The Directorate of Mechanization and Motorization (UMM) and Main Design Bureau of the Arms Arsenal Trust (*Glavnoye Konstruktorskoye Byuro Orudiyno-Oruzheynogo Tresta*, GKB OAT) developed requirements for a much heavier tank than what Tukhachevksiy envisioned back in 1929. This tank would weigh 60-80 tons, have armor up to 50 mm, and still keep a relatively high speed of 25-30 kph. This tank would be armed

---

[24] Ye. Belash, *Tanki Mezhvoyennogo Perioda*, Tactical Press, Moscow, 2014. p.58-59
[25] *Verkhovniy Sovet Narodnogo Khoziaystva*, VSNKh
[26] N. Barinov, *Pochemu podschet tankov malo govorit o moschi armii*, https://zen.yandex.ru/media/id/5ba87f4e1c5a9600aa6b87d6/pochemu-podschet-tankov-malo-govorit-o-mosci-armii--5bc6415fcf1f9400abd53549 retrieved on July 17th, 2022
[27] RGAE F.2097 Op.1 D.1077 L.19 (reverse)-20

with two 76 mm cannons and six machine guns.[28] Due to its extreme weight, it would not be able to use most bridges, and would therefore have to either be able to ford deep rivers or float across them. The Experimental Design and Machinebuilding Department of the Bolshevik factory (OKMO: *Opytno-konstruktorskiy Mekhanicheskiy Otdel*) developed the T-30 tank to meet these requirements. A draft and a wooden model were ready in early 1932. This tank deviated from the UMM's requirements slightly. It would weigh 50 tons and have 45-60 mm of armor. Instead of two 76 mm guns, it would be armed with one 76 mm gun, one 37 mm gun, and six machine guns, operated by a crew of 10. Either a 730 or 850 hp engine would provide the tank with a top speed of 30 kph. Work stalled at this point.[29] This did not deter the Bolshevik factory from working on even more impressive tanks, for instance K.K. Sirken's 85 ton tank armed with a 107 mm gun with a limited traverse, two 45 mm guns in individual turrets, and a 76 mm AA gun in a rear turret. This tank would have up to 80 mm of armor and a 1500 hp engine would provide the required speed of 30 kph. Not even a model of this tank was built.[30]

Foreign Designs and Designers

Without any success from domestic designers, the Directorate of Mechanization and Motorization (UMM) turned to foreign ones. The Italian Ansaldo company was one of several to answer the call. Ansaldo developed a 65-70 ton heavy tank with an original suspension and electric transmission. A full scale model of the tank was built by January of 1933, but the USSR declined the project. That is not to say it was not interested, as materials obtained from Ansaldo were transferred over to

---

[28] A.G. Solyankin and others, *Sovietskiye Tyazheliye Tanki 1917-1941*, Tseyghaus, Moscow, 2006, p.5
[29] A.G. Solyankin and others, *Sovietskiye Tyazheliye Tanki 1917-1941*, Tseyghaus, Moscow, 2006. p.5
[30] A.G. Solyankin and others, *Sovietskiye Tyazheliye Tanki 1917-1941*, Tseyghaus, Moscow, 2006, p.7

the Experimental Design and Machinebuilding Department (OKMO). Another high profile foreign contributor was German engineer Eduard Grote. He was invited to the USSR to work on the TG (Tank Grotte) medium tank at the Bolshevik factory. In addition to work on this tank, he proposed several other projects, a 1000 ton tank for coastal defense being the most famous.[31] This proposal overshadowed the much more reasonable G.D.6 tank. At a weight of 70-75 tons, the G.D.6 would have up to 60-70 mm of armor and three cannons (two 45 mm, one 76 or 100 mm) as well as six machine guns. The tank could reach a speed of 30 kph with an 850 hp engine. This tank was followed by the 100 ton T-42 tank. The T-42 would have up to 70 mm of armor, a 107 mm gun in a central turret, a front turret with a 76 mm gun, and a rear turret with a 45 mm gun. Like Ansaldo's proposal, this tank was rejected, but work on this vehicle laid a foundation for the design of future tanks.[32]

Documentation from the Ansaldo tank, G.D.6, and T-42 was transferred to a design group located at the new Special Machinebuilding Trust (*Spetsialniy Mashinostroitelniy Trest* or *SpetsMashTrest* for short) experimental factory in Leningrad (later renamed factory #185) led by N.V. Barykov. Barykov's group was given the objective to develop a 35 ton breakthrough tank. The result of this work was the T-35.[33] This five-turreted vehicle might have looked unconventional by today's standards, but it met the requirements of the time. Multi-turreted tanks were not uncommon, for instance the British built the five-turreted A1E1 Independent and three turreted Cruiser Tank Mk.I around that time, the Germans built the three-turreted Neubaufahrzeug, and the Americans had several types of two-turreted tanks including the Light Tank M2.[34] The armor of the 37.5 ton T-35 tank did not exceed 30 mm,

[31] Y. Pasholok, *Zhelezniy kaput*, https://warspot.ru/11521-zheleznyy-kaput, retrieved on July 29th, 2022
[32] A.G. Solyankin and others, *Sovietskiye Tyazheliye Tanki 1917-1941*, Tseyghaus, Moscow, 2006. pp. 5-6.
[33] Y. Pasholok, *Peremennaya bronetankovaya terminologiya*, https://dzen.ru/a/YGCuw9h6cDO8KQyZ?&, retrieved on September 27th, 2022
[34] R.P. Hunnicutt, *Stuart A History of the American Light Tank Volume 1*, Presidio Press, 1992. p. 98

but this was enough to withstand contemporary anti-tank guns. Its own armament consisting of one 76 mm gun, two 37 mm guns, and four machine guns was also competitive. A 500 hp M-17 gasoline engine provided this tank with sufficient mobility. The Red Army had finally found a reasonable heavy tank that could meet both its needs and the abilities of the Soviet tank industry.[35]

Five Types of Tanks (1933)

This success was sealed with decree #71ss[36]/o[37] of the Council of Labour and Defense (*Soyuz Truda i Oborony*, STO) of the USSR titled "On the RKKA's [*Raboche-krestyanskaya Krasnaya Armiya*, Worker and Peasant Red Army] system of tank armament" published on August 13th, 1933. This decree defined five types of tanks. The first was the Reconnaissance Tank (*razvedyvatelniy tank*), defined by high speed, a low profile, and low cost. This tank had to be able to maneuver on all terrain, including water. The second type of tank was the Combined Arms Tank (*obschevoyskovoy tank*). This was the main type of tank intended to fight alongside infantry. Mechanized units had their own tank, the Operational Tank (*operativniy tank*). This third type of tank was faster than the Combined Arms Tank and also amphibious. The fourth type of tank had a much more impressive title: Quality Reinforcement Tank of the Tank Reserve of the Supreme Command (*tank kachestvennogo usileniya tankovogo rezerva glavnokomanduyushego*). This tank was meant to break through enemy fortifications. If necessary, it had to be fast enough to keep up with mechanized units. Finally, the fifth type of tank was called the Powerful Special Purpose Tank (*moschniy tank osobogo naznacheniya*). This tank would be used to break

---

[35] A.G. Solyankin and others, *Sovietskiye Tyazheliye Tanki 1917-1941*, Tseyghaus, Moscow, 2006. pp. 8-10

[36] "ss" stands for *sovershenno sekretno* (top secret).

[37] Classification codes in the USSR were limited to [none], *s*, and *ss*. It is thought that any letters in addition to these are notation of the filing system. It is thought that *o* possibly stands for *osoboy [vazhnosti]* (of special [importance]).

through especially tough defensive lines and fortifications. It would have to have powerful weapons and armor thick enough to protect against small caliber artillery.[38]

The decree also defined what types of tanks would match each category. The T-37 filled the reconnaissance tank slot, the T-26 was the combined arms tank, the BT was the operational tank, the T-28 was the Quality Reinforcement Tank (*tank kachestvennogo usileniya*) and the T-35 filled the role of the Powerful Special Purpose Tank (*moschniy tank osobogo nazhnacheniya*).[39]

Despite this assignment, the decree notes that Soviet tank forces had to keep evolving and already called for improvements to existing designs. The T-35 was due to be replaced by a superior special purpose tank by the end of the second Five Year Plan in 1937.[40] That is not to say that the Red Army was satisfied with the T-35 as it was first envisioned. The production variant had up to 50 mm of armor and 45 mm guns instead of 37 mm ones, increasing its weight to 50 tons. An 800 hp engine was needed to keep the power to weight ratio within reasonable parameters.[41] Such an engine was never produced, but the tank only kept getting heavier. Thanks to various modernizations the T-35 reached a mass of 55 tons by the time it was taken out of production in 1939.[42]

It was clear that the T-35 was obsolete long before that. Komkor (corps commander) Dmitry Pavlov, chief of the Automotive and Armored Vehicle Directorate (ABTU: *Avto-bronetankovoye Upravleniye*) sent a letter to People's Commissar of Defense Marshal Kliment Voroshilov on February 21st, 1938, listing his thoughts on the status of the Red Army's

---

[38] GA RF F.R-8418 Op.28 D.2 L.72-79
[39] A.G. Solyankin and others, *Sovietskiye Tyazheliye Tanki 1917-1941*, Tseyghaus, Moscow, 2006. p.8
[40] GA RF F.R-8418 Op.28 D.2 L.72-79
[41] RGAE F.7297 Op.38 D.32 L.10
[42] A.G. Solyankin and others, *Sovietskiye Tyazheliye Tanki 1917-1941*, Tseyghaus, Moscow, 2006. p.12

tanks. According to him, the T-35 was no longer suitable for its role as a heavy breakthrough tank. Its armor was vulnerable to 37 mm guns at ranges under 1000 meters and to 45 mm guns at ranges under 2000 meters. A modern breakthrough tank required 50-55 mm of armor to resist these weapons at all ranges. It was impossible to increase the T-35's armor any further, as the vehicle exceeded its modernization reserve long ago. A brand new heavy tank was needed.[43]

Replacing the T-35

Requirements for the new heavy tank were composed on August 7th, 1938, at a meeting of the Committee of Defense within the Council of Commissars of the USSR (*Komitet oborony pri sovete kommissarov SSSR*). Despite a need for a revolutionary leap, the new heavy tank was oddly reminiscent of the T-35. It was to have a single 76 mm gun, two 45 mm guns, and three machine guns. With armor up to 60 mm thick, its mass was estimated at 55-57 tons. The task of developing this tank was given to two factories: the Kirov Factory in Leningrad (*Leningradskiy Kirovskiy Zavod*, LKZ) and factory #185. The factories submitted rival designs: the former named their tank SMK after Sergey Mironovich Kirov, a popular Soviet politician. The latter gave their tank a more mundane name: T-100.[44] The tanks did not cling to their obsolete heritage for long. Models of the SMK and T-100 were presented at a meeting of the Committee of Defense held on December 9th, 1938. According to the official story, Stalin was personally responsible for removing one of the turrets with a 45 mm gun, famously quipping: "Don't make a supermarket out of your tank".[45] Stalin allegedly also expressed a desire for a single-turreted tank at this meeting. It is impossible to say whether or not this exchange actually took place at the meeting, but either way both the SMK and T-100 were built with just two turrets: a large one with a 76 mm gun and

---

[43] RGVA F.4 Op.19 D.55 L.1-9
[44] M. Kolomiyets, *Leningradskiye KV*, Tactical Press, Moscow, 2013. p.5
[45] N.S. Popov and others, *Konstruktor Boyevykh Mashin*, Lenizdat, Leningrad, 1988, p.69

a small one with a 45 mm gun. Only the LKZ followed Stalin's alleged request and produced a tank with one turret. This tank was named KV after Kliment Voroshilov. Requirements for this tank were composed on December 9th, 1938, and signed by Voroshilov on February 19th or 20th, 1939. Specialized Design Bureau #2 (SKB-2: *Spetsializirovannoye Konstruktorskoye Byuro 2*) at LKZ began working on the tank even before that, on February 1st, 1939.[46] The new tank would be a radical improvement over its multi-turreted predecessors. The armor was increased to 75 mm all-around at a weight of just 40 tons.[47]

The KV-1

Despite its revolutionary design, the KV was destined to repeat the fate of its ancestor. The U-0 prototype already surpassed the initial weight requirement, coming in at 42 tons,[48] and the first production KV tanks with a small turret mounting a 76 mm L-11 gun (later renamed KV-1) weighed 44 tons. This mass only increased as various improvements were requested. Tanks with 76mm F-32 guns built starting in early 1941 already weighed 47 tons.[49] This was undesirable, but not uncommon; for instance, the A-34 prototype tank weighed 25.6 tons when it was accepted into service in March of 1940, but by the end of the year the production T-34 tank already weighed 26.7 tons,[50] and T-34 tanks produced in 1942 weighed more than 28 tons.[51] This tendency was not unique to Soviet tanks, either. The Medium Tank T6 prototype built in

[46] TsAMO RF F.38 Op.11355 D.934 L.1
[47] M. Kolomiyets, *Leningradskiye KV*, Tactical Press, Moscow, 2013. p.10
[48] Y. Pasholok, *Ne Poletevshiy Kak Lastochka*, https://zen.yandex.ru/media/yuripasholok/ne-poletevshii-kak-lastochka-60114787a3e47e7ee8bf5db4. Retrieved on May 9th, 2021
[49] A.G. Solyankin and others, *Sovietskiye Tyazheliye Tanki 1917-1941*, Tseyghaus, Moscow, 2006. pp.28-29
[50] TsAMO RF F.38 Op.11355 D.41 L.10-11
[51] Y. Pasholok, *Vremennoye Usilieniye*, https://warspot.ru/12390-vremennoe-usilenie, retrieved on December 23rd, 2021

1941 weighed 27 tons,[52] the Medium Tank M4A1 already weighed 30.3 tons when it entered production in 1942, and upgrades such as the 76 mm gun and a new turret drove its weight up to 32.1 tons by 1944.[53] Similarly, the German Pz.Kpfw.IV Ausf.A produced in 1936 weighed 18.3 tons, the Pz.Kpfw.IV Ausf.D produced in 1940 already weighed 20.3 tons, and the Pz.Kpfw.IV Ausf.H that entered production in 1943 weighed 25.4 tons.[54]

This weight increase was partially driven by an arms race with the Germans. Intelligence reports of German heavy tanks with guns as large as 105 mm in caliber prompted another series of improvements, most notably thicker armor.[55] Applique plates 25-30 mm thick were bolted or welded onto the hull and turret, which also impacted the weight. The turret armor thickness was later increased to 90 mm, which allowed some weight savings compared to the two-layer design. However, the deficit in armor plates of the proper thickness due to the start of the Great Patriotic War led to installation of hull applique armor made from any available plates, which were often considerably thicker than the authorized plates, sometimes as thick as 90 mm. This emergency measure drove up the mass of the tanks even higher.[56]

Wartime pressures meant that the tanks had to be cheaper and faster to produce. This led to the replacement of aluminium parts with heavier but cheaper iron and steel equivalents.[57] The introduction of cast turrets with up to 100-110 mm thick armor also contributed to increased weight, as did the longer 76 mm ZIS-5 gun (*Zavod imeni Stalina*, ZIS – Stalin Factory) with a thicker gun mantlet. All in all, a KV-1 tank

---

[52] Y. Pasholok, *Na puti k samomu massovomu amerikanskomu tanku*, https://warspot.ru/17313-na-puti-k-samomu-massovomu-amerikanskomu-tanku, retrieved on February 16th, 2022

[53] P. Ware, *M4 Sherman Tank 1941 Onwards All Variants*, Zenith Press, 2012, p.34

[54] T. Anderson, *Panzer IV*, Osprey Publishing, 2021, pp. 33, 71, 226

[55] TsAMO RF F.38 Op.11355 D.895 L.9

[56] M. Kolomiyets, *Tyazheliy Tank KV-1 Perviye Tanki Pobedy*, Eksmo, Moscow, 2017. pp.54-55

[57] M. Kolomiyets, *Tyazheliy Tank KV-1 Perviye Tanki Pobedy*, Eksmo, Moscow, 2017. pp.83

produced at the Kirov Factory in Chelyabinsk (ChKZ for short, an amalgamation of the Chelyabinsk Tractor Factory and evacuated elements of LKZ) in the winter of 1941-1942 could easily weigh 50 tons, if not more. The extra weight increased the strain on the tanks' engine, transmission, and running gear, reducing the reliability of the tanks. Mobility also suffered. This was especially noticeable in the winter, when KV-1 tanks had to traverse deep snow. This matter was raised by Stalin in a conversation with People's Commissar of Tank Production Vyacheslav Aleksandrovich Malyshev.[58] On January 24th, 1942, Stalin personally tasked Isaac Moiseyevich Zaltsman, formerly the director of LKZ (Kirov Factory in Leningrad) and now the head of the newly formed group of factories nicknamed Tankograd, to resolve these issues.[59] There were two methods of improving the tank's mobility and reliability: installation of more powerful engines and a reduction in weight. The former approach proved fruitless. The initial bold proposal to start using 700 hp engines ran into issues, as even a 650 hp engine proved too much for the tank's cooling system. Even reduction of the tank's weight ordered on February 23rd, 1942, was just a bandaid solution. According to State Committee of Defense (*Gosudarstvenniy Komitet Oborony*, GKO) decree #1331ss Kirov factory would produce tanks without external fuel tanks, with racks for only 90 rounds of ammunition for the main gun, reduced number of tools carried on board, and new tracks where only every other link had a guide horn.[60] These measures resulted in a reduction in weight of 1.3 tons, which was only a small step towards the mass the tank had in its initial state. Decree #1332ss issued on the same day ordered strict control to be established over armor components, mandating the thickness of cast turrets to remain within 95-100 mm.[61] These measures reduced the weight of a KV-1 tank to 47 tons by May of 1942.[62] Zaltsman and Chief Designer of the Chelyabinsk Kirov

[58] Y. Pasholok, *Ne Poletevshiy Kak Lastochka*, https://zen.yandex.ru/media/yuripasholok/ne-poletevshii-kak-lastochka-60114787a3e47e7ee8bf5db4. Retrieved on May 9th, 2021
[59] TsAMO RF F.38 Op.11355 D.958 L.8
[60] RGASPI F.644 Op.1 D.22 L.6
[61] M. Kolomiyets, *Tyazheliy Tank KV-1 Perviye Tanki Pobedy*, Eksmo, Moscow, 2017. pp.93-98
[62] M. Kolomiyets, *Tyazheliy Tank KV-1 Perviye Tanki Pobedy*, Eksmo, Moscow, 2017. pp.105

Factory (ChKZ) Josef Kotin had little faith in these half-measures from the start, predicting that reduction in weight of 2-3 tons would not give the desired effect.[63]

The Red Army had another heavy tank, the KV-2. This tank equipped with a 152 mm M-10 howitzer in an enlarged turret was developed in 1940 to deal with Finnish fortifications.[64] The larger turret and gun increased the weight of this vehicle to 54 tons. A lighter turret was developed by October of 1940, reducing its weight to 52 tons.[65] This tank was taken out of production in June of 1941 and was therefore not affected by either the wartime pressures that caused the KV-1 to gain weight or the weight reduction measures introduced in early 1942.[66]

The KV-1S

The third decree issued by the State Committee of Defense (*Gosudarstvenniy Komitet Oborony*, GKO) on February 23rd, 1942, marked the start of a longer journey. Decree #1334ss required the production of a heavy tank weighing 45-45.5 tons.[67] This kind of leeway in weight limits is not uncommon and could be found in other requirements, for example the T-34-85 tank accepted into service in 1943 could weigh between 32 and 32.5 tons.[68] This decree led to some more measures to reduce the weight and improve mobility of the tank, but a real change in direction came on June 5th, 1942, with GKO decree #1878ss. This decree required ChKZ (Kirov Factory in Chelyabinsk) to

---

[63] M. Kolomiyets, *Tyazheliy Tank KV-1 Perviye Tanki Pobedy*, Eksmo, Moscow, 2017. pp.93
[64] A.G. Solyankin and others, *Sovietskiye Tyazheliye Tanki 1917-1941*, Tseyghaus, Moscow, 2006. p.31
[65] A.G. Solyankin and others, *Sovietskiye Tyazheliye Tanki 1917-1941*, Tseyghaus, Moscow, 2006. p.40
[66] I. Afonin, *Svodka Tankovogo upravleniya Glavnogo bronetankovogo upravleniya "O nalichii tankov v Krasnoj Armii za period s 1 yanvarya 1941 goda po 1 yanvarya 1944 goda"*, https://dentankista2018.mil.ru/, retrieved on December 23rd, 2021
[67] M. Kolomiyets, *Tyazheliy Tank KV-1 Perviye Tanki Pobedy*, Eksmo, Moscow, 2017. pp.98
[68] RGASPI F.644 Op.2 D.320 L.110

produce a radically lighter tank weighing just 42.5 tons. This reduction in weight came at the cost of armor: the sides and lower front of the hull were thinned out from 75 to 60 mm, the thickness of turret armor was reduced to 80-85 mm, all applique armor was removed.[69] This tank also had some improvements such as a new 8-speed gearbox and commander's cupola.[70] Interestingly enough, this change in armor thickness and features did not change in how the tanks were organized or used. Both types of tanks were used simultaneously in heavy tank breakthrough regiments.[71] Production of this new tank, dubbed KV-1S, was just another half-measure. It was obvious that the age of the KV tank was at an end. The Red Army's first indigenous heavy tank stayed in production for six years, but its successor needed to be replaced entirely after just two and a half.

---

[69] RGASPI F.644 Op.2 D.69 L.71-76
[70] A.G. Solyankin and others, *Sovetskiye tyazheliye tanki 1941-1945*, Tseyghaus, Moscow, 2007 pp.37-39
[71] RGVA F.4 Op.12 D.106 L.112-122

The First IS Tanks

The need for a new heavy tank was not a surprise to SKB-2 (*Spetsializirovannoye Konstruktorskoye Byuro 2*, Specialized Design Bureau #2) staff, and work on a conceptually novel tank was already underway. In March of 1942, Nikolai Valentinovich Tseits, a seasoned tank designer, was appointed as the senior engineer on a new tank project indexed KV-13. The objective was a difficult one: to obtain a tank with the mass of a T-34 and the armor of a KV-1.[72] Requirements composed by the Main Automotive and Armored Vehicle Directorate (*Glavnoye Avto-bronetankovoye Upravleniye*, GABTU) called for a 30 ton tank with 90 mm thick frontal armor and 75 mm thick side armor. A correction was made to these requirements in pencil: 85-120 mm thick front hull and turret armor and a mass of 34-35 tons.[73] The use of a 500 hp V-2 or 600 hp V-2K engine was expected. The top speed of this tank would have been impressive: 60 kph, faster than not only the KV-1, but also the T-34. When experimental factory #100 was split off from ChKZ (Kirov Factory in Chelyabinsk), the work was partially transferred to the newly formed Special Design Bureau (SKB) at factory #100. As Tseits was a superstitious man, he lobbied to change his tank's unlucky name. He succeeded, but only partially. While ChKZ continued to refer to the project as KV-13, there was a new name for it at factory #100: IS-1. Both factories assigned the tank the blueprint index 233.[74] For the sake of simplicity, the index KV-13 will be used in this book to refer to this vehicle.

---

[72] TsAMO RF F.38 Op.11355 D.935 L.184-186
[73] RGASPI F.644 Op.2 D.69 L.71-76
[74] Y. Pasholok, *Perviy KV Pod Neschastlivym Nomerom, https://warspot.ru/9279-pervyy-kv-pod-neschastlivym-nomerom, retrieved on May 10th, 2021*

The KV-13

Development of the KV-13 was well underway by the time GKO (State Committee of Defense) decree #1878ss was drafted. Paragraphs 9 and 10 list updated requirements. The new KV-13 was required to have up to 100 mm of front armor and 80-85 mm thick sides. It would have the same 600 hp V-2K engine that the KV-1 had, but at a weight of just 35 tons the top speed increased to 50 kph. The reduced crew (now only a commander doubling as a radio operator, gunner, loader, and driver) suggested that the reduction in weight came as a consequence of a radical change in layout. However, it was not to be. Stalin crossed out paragraphs 9 and 10 before signing the decree.[75] No mention of the KV-13 remained in the final version, signed on June 5th, 1942.[76]

The GKO approved production of two KV-13 prototypes on July 1st 1942, but this did not mean that development would progress smoothly. Two major events affected KV-13 development: one was GKO decree #1958 dated July 3rd, ordering the start of production of T-34 tanks at ChKZ (Kirov Factory in Chelyabinsk), which further strained the factory's limited engineering manpower. The second was a more serious setback: Tseits died from a heart attack on July 19th, 1942. The task of finishing the KV-13 fell to Nikolai Fedorovich Shashmurin, another experienced designer. Shashmurin had a personal distaste for Tseits' project, but nevertheless took up his mantle when work resumed in September of 1942. The hull and turret designs were finished by September 13th, and production of the first prototype began on that same day. Work continued despite a personal order issued by Zaltsman on September 14th prohibiting experimental work at factory #100. The tank was complete by September 26th.[77]

---

[75] RGASPI F.644 Op.2 D.69 L.74
[76] RGASPI F.644 Op.1 D.38 L.260-263
[77] Y. Pasholok, *Perviy KV Pod Neschastlivym Nomerom*, https://warspot.ru/9279-pervyy-kv-pod-neschastlivym-nomerom, retrieved on May 10th, 2021

Despite its index, the KV-13 had little to do with the KV-1. There was a certain visual similarity, but the differences were blatant. The driver was now the sole remaining crewman in the front of the hull, positioned in the center. The road wheels and return rollers were reminiscent of those used in the T-50 tank prototype built at LKZ (Kirov Factory in Leningrad) before the war. The cooling system was also heavily influenced by the T-50. Drive sprockets were closer to those used on the T-34, and track links were taken from the T-34 entirely. The turret was similar to the one used on the KV-1S, but this was also a brand new design.[78]

Trials began on September 26th, 1942 and revealed a wide range of issues, as can be expected with any revolutionary tank. The first outing concluded relatively well, the only defect that showed itself was low oil pressure at high engine RPM. This was corrected by repairs of the oil reductor valve . September 27th brought more trouble. Even though the ambient temperature was 10-12 °C, water temperature in the cooling system reached 110-115 °C. The engine worked poorly in 9th gear. It was difficult to control the tank, as it took up to 60 kg of effort to operate the steering levers and up to 90 to operate the main clutch pedal. Despite these and other defects, the tank was even faster than required. With the engine running at 1800 RPM it reached a top speed of 55 kph.[79] Shashmurin took the driver's seat himself in these trials, and it seemed that he spared no effort in ending the project that he so despised. Taking the tank along a cobblestone road at top speed, he quickly destroyed the experimental road wheels. The KV-13 was put out of commission for a week as wheels were replaced and other defects were ironed out. The newly tuned KV-13 was easier to steer (required effort was reduced to 24 kg from the initial 60 kg). The tank returned to trials on October 5th, but new issues cropped up. The track tensioning mechanism was too weak, and loose tracks flapping up and down at high speed quickly tore off the fenders, after which the air intakes became

[78] Y. Pasholok, *Perviy KV Pod Neschastlivym Nomerom*, https://warspot.ru/9279-pervyy-kv-pod-neschastlivym-nomerom, retrieved on May 10th, 2021
[79] TsAMO RF F.38 Op.11355 D.958 L.109-110

clogged with mud. The tank was once again withdrawn for improvements, returning to the field on October 13th. New gearbox issues were found. All in all, the KV-13 drove for 715 km in September-November of 1942 until it was clear that further trials were senseless. Replacing the drive sprocket and tracks with KV-1S style designs did not help with the tank's technical issues. Trials of the KV-13 continued, but there was no longer any chance of it seeing mass production.[80]

The IS-1 (Early Prototype #233)

Even though the prototype suffered from considerable teething troubles, these trials achieved one important thing. It was conclusively proven that it was possible to build a tank that was both much lighter and much better protected than the KV-1. Work on a radically improved KV-13 began in November of 1942. The draft design was ready by December 10th, 1942.[81] The tank retained its previous names: at factory #100 it was called IS-1, at ChKZ (Kirov Factory in Chelyabinsk) it was called KV-13, both factories used the blueprints index 233. The new tank was also influenced by existing designs. A new three-man turret was installed on the expanded turret ring, now 1590 mm wide . The more compact 76mm F-34[82] gun was used instead of the 76mm ZIS-5, which freed up more room in the fighting compartment. Ammunition racks from both the T-34 and KV-1 were used. A commander's cupola with a PTK-5 periscope and a hatch was added.[83] The running gear was greatly influenced by the KV-1S. The 650 mm wide track links and drive sprockets were used without changes. The road wheels were reduced in diameter to 550 mm, but were otherwise

---

[80] Y. Pasholok, *Perviy KV Pod Neschastlivym Nomerom*, https://warspot.ru/9279-pervyy-kv-pod-neschastlivym-nomerom, retrieved on May 10th, 2021

[81] Y. Pasholok, *Predposledniy Shag*, https://warspot.ru/9483-predposledniy-shag, retrieved on May 12th, 2021

[82] The letter F in the designation indicates that this gun was developed at factory #92 in Gorky.

[83] A.G. Solyankin and others, *Sovietskiye Tyazheliye Tanki 1917-1941*, Tseyghaus, Moscow, 2006. p.92

similar to those already in production. Instead of an original gearbox, the tank had an improved variant of the 8-speed gearbox from the KV-1S.[84] Changes in the design of the hull (including thickening the armor) led to a worrying result. Like other Soviet heavy tanks before it, the KV-13 started to gain weight. The second prototype was now estimated to weigh 37.5 tons. The top speed was expected to remain high at 53.5 kph.[85]

The start of development of the KV-14 (SU-152) SPG delayed work on the new KV-13. Factory #100 was dependent on the Ural Heavy Machinebuilding Factory (*Uralskiy Zavod Tyazhelogo Mashinostroyeniya*, UZTM) for production of armored components, but this factory was now also busy with starting up T-34 and SU-122 production. All internal components for the new KV-13 were finished by February 1st, 1943, but factory #100 was still waiting for the hull and turret to arrive. On February 23rd, 1943, Zaltsman grew tired of waiting. He wrote a letter petitioning Stalin and Molotov to expedite production of the new tank.[86]

GKO (State Committee of Defense) decree #2943ss signed on the next day resolved matters. Two prototypes were now expected for delivery by March 10th, 1943. One tank weighing up to 38.5 tons would be armed with the 76 mm F-34 gun. The other, weighing up to 39.5 tons, would be equipped with the 122 mm U-11 howitzer. Both tanks had up to 120 mm thick front armor and 90 mm thick sides. This was enough to reliably protect the tank frontally from the 75 mm Pak[87] 40 and 88 mm KwK[88] 36, the most powerful German guns known at the time. The tanks' top speed remained high: 55 kph with the 600 hp V-2K engine.

[84] A.G. Solyankin and others, *Sovietskiye Tyazheliye Tanki 1917-1941*, Tseyghaus, Moscow, 2006. p.94
[85] Y. Pasholok, *Predposledniy Shag*, https://warspot.ru/9483-predposledniy-shag, retrieved on May 12th, 2021
[86] RGASPI F.644 Op.2 D.138 L.197
[87] Pak: *Panzerabwehrkanone*, anti-tank gun
[88] KwK: *Kampfwagenkanone*, tank gun

There was another important change: the index KV-13 was no longer in use. These tanks were now called IS-1 and IS-2.[89]

Stalin's approval expedited matters. A hull and a turret arrived by February 27th, and assembly was complete by March 8th. The mass of the IS-1 tank turned out to be lower than expected, 37.1 tons. The first few outings revealed manufacturing defects, but the difference compared to the first KV-13 was like night and day. A new radiator reduced the temperature of the water in the cooling system to 50°C at an ambient temperature of 15°C. The tank managed to reach its required top speed of 55 kph. There were still improvements needed. For instance, the trials commission requested that the loader be given a MK-IV periscope (Soviet copy of the Vickers Tank Periscope Mk.IV, in turn a copy of the Gundlach periscope) and the driver be given two of them to improve observation. There were some criticisms of the commander's cupola and the gun mount. The tank's reduced length compared to the KV-1 resulted in the reduction of road wheels from six to five per side, which increased ground pressure. The commission required the return of the sixth road wheel. Finally, the problem with mud flying up onto the air intakes was not fully resolved. None of these issues were impossible to correct and it seemed like the tank was well on its way towards being accepted into service. ChKZ (Kirov Factory in Chelyabinsk) began preparing for the production of a pilot batch of 10 tanks.[90]

The IS-2 (Early Prototype #234)

The IS-1 was not the only tank mentioned in decree #2943ss. The other prototype that was approved for production was the IS-2 tank with

---

[89] RGASPI F.644 Op.2 D.138 L.194-196
[90] Y. Pasholok, *Predposledniy Shag*, https://warspot.ru/9483-predposledniy-shag, retrieved on May 12th, 2021

blueprint index 234. This tank had the same hull, but a different turret mounting the 122 mm U-11 howitzer.

The idea of a 122 mm howitzer in a heavy tank was nothing new. It was first born in the fall of 1941 when KV-1 production was first being set up at ChKZ (Kirov Factory in Chelyabinsk) after evacuation from Leningrad.[91] The only remaining source of 76 mm tank guns was factory #92 in Gorky, more than 1000 km away. This posed a risk, and the People's Commissariat of Tank Production (*Narodniy Kommissariat Tankovoy Promyshlennosti*, NKTP) searched for a solution. It seemed preferable to use a locally sourced gun, and such an option was available. Production of the 122 mm M-30[92] howitzer began at the Ural Heavy Machinebuilding Factory (UZTM) back in 1940. F.F. Petrov, the gun's original designer, remained in Sverdlovsk as UZTM's chief designer after overseeing assembly line setup. Having him develop a tank gun based on the towed variant of his weapon seemed like the ideal option. A design of such a gun, indexed U-11, was presented at a meeting held in late November of 1941. A prototype was finished by the end of the year and installed in a tank in January of 1942. This tank received a new index: KV-9. Trials held in February of 1942 ended on a positive note, but by the time they ended Factory #8 was evacuated to Sverdlovsk and began production of 76 mm ZIS-5 guns there. The threat to the KV-1's supply chain was gone and the KV-9 project died, since there was no longer a need to produce an alternative gun. The KV-9 is often compared to the KV-2, but it is important to make a distinction between these two howitzer-armed tanks. While the KV-2 was equipped with its howitzer specifically to tackle Finnish fortifications, the KV-9 was only equipped with a howitzer because it was readily available, rather than for a specific mission.[93]

---

[91] Y. Pasholok, *Bolshaya Pushka dlya Nebolshoy Bashni*, https://warspot.ru/8778-bolshaya-pushka-dlya-nebolshoy-bashni, retrieved on May 15th, 2021
[92] The letter M in the designation indicates that the howitzer was developed at factory #172 in Motovilikha.
[93] Y. Pasholok, *Gaubichniy KV*, https://warspot.ru/9026-gaubichnyy-kv, retrieved on May 15th, 2021

Even though the KV-9 was not put into mass production, its U-11 howitzer was not without merit. The high explosive effect of the 122 mm shell was superior to that of the 76 mm shell. In addition to having a heavier casing that created more lethal fragments upon detonation, the larger shell carried more explosive filler: 3.675 kg in the 122 mm OF[94]-462 shell[95] compared to 1.08 kg in the 76 mm OF-350 shell.[96] A 76 mm HE shell fired with a delayed fuse and bursting in soil of medium density created a crater half a meter deep and one meter across, while a 122 mm shell exploding in the same manner made a crater 0.7 meters deep and 3 meters across.[97] Reduced penetration of the AP shell compared to the 76 mm gun meant that the weapon had no chance of becoming the gun of the main Soviet heavy tank, but it could still be used on artillery support tanks.[98] This argument was considered sufficient to authorize an offshoot of the new heavy tank program, although the priority of the IS-1 was still higher. As the work began before official authorization was received, the prototype was finished on March 12th, 1943. The only thing that remained in common with the KV-9 was the U-11 howitzer. Even though the turret was visually similar, it was an original design. The armor of the new turret was thicker than that of its predecessor, but the overall weight was reduced from 9.2 to 7.4 tons. Weighing of the prototype showed that it weighed 37.9 tons, considerably less than expected.[99] Like the IS-1, the IS-2 had a four man crew: a driver in the hull and a loader, gunner, and commander in the turret. The turret also housed 8 rounds of ammunition, 30 more were located in the hull. Trials showed that the extra 800 kg of weight did not impact the tank's mobility or reliability, as the performance of

---

[94] OF: *oskolochno-fugasniy*, fragmentation-high explosive
[95] *Tablitsy strelby 122-mm gaubitsy obr. 1938 g.*, 5th annotated edition, Military Publisher of the People's Commissariat of Defense, Moscow, 1943 p.8
[96] *Kratkiye tablitsy strelby 76-mm pushki obr. 1941 g. (ZIS-3)*, Military Publisher of the People's Commissariat of Defense, Moscow, 1942 p.18
[97] N.N. Nikiforov and others, *Artilleriya*, 5th edition, Military Publisher of the Ministry of Defense, Moscow, 1953 p.133
[98] Y. Pasholok, Gaubichniy KV, https://warspot.ru/9026-gaubichnyy-kv, retrieved on May 15th, 2021
[99] TsAMO RF F. 38 Op.11355 D.1401 L.18-21

the two tanks was the same.[100] The biggest criticism was related to the loader's workspace. The trials commission concluded that the production tank should have a turret ring that was 150 mm wider. The same comment was made regarding the IS-1. The idea of putting a 122 mm howitzer on a heavy tank turned out to be perfectly feasible.[101]

---

[100] TsAMO RF F.38 Op.11355 D.1660 L.12
[101] Y. Pasholok, *Pervoye Prishestviye IS-1*, https://warspot.ru/9911-pervoe-prishestvie-is-2, retrieved on May 15th. 2021

Tiger Killers

A British intelligence memo sent on October 7th, 1942, warned the USSR about new types of German tanks.[102] One of the tanks mentioned in the memo was indexed Pz.Kpfw.VI. Little was known about it except that it was likely heavier than the Pz.Kpfw.III and Pz.Kpfw.IV. Unbeknownst to the Red Army, this new tank was already on the front lines. Its arrival at Mga (a town in Leningrad Oblast) on August 29th, 1942, went unnoticed as the Tigers failed to achieve any impact. In an attack on September 22nd, 1942, all four Tigers employed with the s.Pz.Abt.502[103] were lost in battle with the Soviet 2nd Shock Army. Three tanks were recovered, but the fourth vehicle remained in no man's land.[104] Soviet scouts showed no interest in it and made no attempt to inspect the previously unseen tank.[105] The new German tank would not remain a secret for long, as the next Soviet attempt to penetrate the blockade around Leningrad required their intervention. Two tanks belonging to the s.Pz.Abt.502 were lost on January 17th, but the Germans managed to demolish them.[106] They were not so lucky on the next day, as the Red Army captured two intact tanks at Workers' Village #5.[107]

Analyzing the Tiger

Even preliminary inspections showed that these tanks had radically thicker armor than their predecessors. The tanks were shipped to the Armored Vehicle Scientific Research Proving Grounds (*Nauchno-Issledovatelniy Bronetankoviy Poligon*, NIBT Proving Grounds) at Kubinka where one tank was subjected to penetration trials between April 25th

---

[102] Y. Pasholok, *Tyazheliy trofey s Kurskoy dugi*, https://warspot.ru/10672-tyazhyolyy-trofey-s-kurskoy-dugi, retrieved on May 24th, 2021
[103] s.Pz.Abt.502: *schwere Panzer Abteilung 502*, 502nd Heavy Tank Battalion
[104] W. Schneider, *Tigers in Combat I*, Stackpole Books, Mechanicsburg, 2004 p.73
[105] A. Ulanov, D. Shein, *Perviye Tridtsatchetverki*, Tactical Press, Moscow, 2014 p.35
[106] W. Schneider, *Tigers in Combat I*, Stackpole Books, Mechanicsburg, 2004 p.75
[107] N.S. Popov and others, *Konstruktor Boyevykh Mashin*, Lenizdat, Leningrad, 1988, p. 255

and April 30th, 1943.[108] These trials confirmed the worst: the 76 mm gun was completely inadequate for fighting this type of tank. While some improvement could be obtained by development of new types of ammunition, it was time to start looking at larger calibers.[109] The 122 mm howitzer used in trials did not score any fair hits on the tank, but prior trials showed that HE shells did not penetrate even a 76 mm thick plate and the AP shell could only match the penetration of the 76 mm gun at the cost of exceeding acceptable pressure in the chamber.[110] It was clear that neither of the two prospective Soviet heavy tanks were capable of fighting the new German Tiger tank.

Thankfully, the Red Army had a solid reserve of anti-tank weapons. 85 mm model 1939 AA (52-K)[111] guns were successfully deployed in battle as ersatz anti-tank guns as early as the fall of 1941.[112] These guns also took part in the penetration trials held in April of 1943. The 85 mm 52-K firing an armor piercing shell penetrated the side of the tank from a range of up to 1450 meters, causing large breaches in the armor. The front plate was penetrated once from 1000 meters. A shot from 1500 meters did not penetrate, but a second shot fired at the same range shattered the Tiger's armor, knocking off a large chunk. This gun made for a more promising weapon than the 76 mm F-34 or ZIS-5.[113]

Upgunning the IS

The response from the GBTU (Main Armored Vehicle Directorate) was quick. Requirements for a new IS tank were defined on May 4th,

---

[108] TsAMO RF F.38 Op.11377 D.12 L.1a
[109] TsAMO RF F.38 Op.11377 D.12 L.25
[110] Y. Pasholok, *Pervoye Prishestviye IS-1*, https://warspot.ru/9911-pervoe-prishestvie-is-2, retrieved on May 15th. 2021
[111] The letter K in the designation indicates that the gun was designed at factory #8 in Kalinin.
[112] RGASPI F.644 Op.2 D.21 L.80
[113] TsAMO RF F.38 Op.11377 D.12 L.33

1943.[114] This tank was a departure from the existing IS-1 and IS-2. The crew was once again increased to 5 men. The required turret ring diameter increased to 1800 mm to fit a turret large enough to house the new 85 mm gun with ballistics of the 52-K AA gun. 60 rounds of 85 mm ammunition would be carried. The armor remained about the same: 120 mm thick front and 90 mm thick sides. The mass of the new tank was estimated to be 43-44 tons. With the existing V-2K engine the expected top speed dropped to 35-37 kph.[115] The requirement for a heavy tank with an 85 mm gun was echoed by the GKO (State Committee of Defense) on the next day.[116]

Luckily, work on 85 mm tank guns did not have to start from scratch. The first requirements for a tank gun of this caliber were dated June 21st, 1940, when orders were given to begin work on the installation of an 85 mm gun into the turret of a KV tank and a turreted tank destroyer on the T-34 chassis.[117] The work was urgent, and the experimental 85 mm F-30 gun was developed by Vasily Gavrilovich Grabin's design group at factory #92 and tested in a T-28 tank in September of 1940. This gun was never installed in a KV tank, but it was tested in the KV-1's potential replacement: the T-220.[118] The F-30 was considered unsatisfactory and canceled in favor of the 107 mm ZIS-6 tank gun.[119]

Grabin did not give up on making an 85 mm tank gun. Another attempt was made in October of 1942 with the same objective: to build an 85 mm tank gun while reusing as many existing parts as possible. The new gun was called ZIS-25. Again, this project was declined, this time due to

---

[114] TsAMO RF F.38 Op.11355 D.1380 L.185-186
[115] TsAMO RF F.38 Op.11355 D.1380 L.185-186
[116] RGASPI F.644 Op.1 D.113 L.49
[117] Y. Pasholok, *Sovetskiye Istrebiteli Tankov s Krugovym Obstrelom*, https://warspot.ru/4819-u-20-sovetskie-istrebiteli-tankov-s-krugovym-obstrelom, retrieved on May 5th, 2021
[118] Y. Pasholok, *Opytniy Tank s Boyevoy Biografiyey*, https://warspot.ru/4884-opytnyy-tank-s-boevoy-biografiey, retrieved on May 15th, 2021
[119] Y. Pasholok, *Krupniy kalibr dlya krupnykh KV*, https://zen.yandex.ru/media/yuripasholok/krupnyi-kalibr-dlia-krupnyh-kv-5ff34325af142f0b17d2cf6c, retrieved on August 17th, 2022

the projected reduction in the rate of fire.[120] While the gun could fit into the production turret of the KV-1 tank, the loader would have difficulty working with the long 85 mm rounds.[121] Work on the ZIS-25 was not done in vain, as the Central Artillery Design Bureau (*Tsentralnoye Artilleriyskoye Konstruktorskoye Byuro*, TsAKB) used it as a starting point to develop the S-31 85 mm tank gun in May of 1943. The advantage of this gun was not only that it recycled 85% of its parts from the ZIS-5, but also that it could fit into the existing turret ring of the IS-1, although it still needed a new turret.[122]

Object 238, an upgrade to the KV-1S tank that would make it competitive against the new German Tiger tank. The 85 mm gun S-31 gun had the ballistics of the 52-K AA gun. Patriot Park museum. (*Pavel Borovikov*)

[120] TsAMO RF F.38 Op.11355 D.697 L.27
[121] Y. Pasholok, *Bolshaya Pushka dlya Nebolshoy Bashni*, https://warspot.ru/8778-bolshaya-pushka-dlya-nebolshoy-bashni, retrieved on May 15th, 2021
[122] Y. Pasholok, *Predposledniy Shag*, https://warspot.ru/9483-predposledniy-shag, retrieved on May 16th, 2021

This was not the only lineage of 85 mm tank guns developed in the USSR. UZTM (Ural Heavy Machinebuilding Factory) developed a potential replacement for the ZIS-5 called U-12 back in 1941. The U-12 had the ballistics of the 85 mm 52-K AA gun, but a new recoil system that would shorten the recoil to 450 mm, making it suitable for installation in a tank.[123] Unlike the U-11, it was never built, but the idea of building an 85 mm tank gun persisted at factory #8. The factory's designers received the same objective as Grabin: fit an 85 mm gun into the ZIS-5 mount while preserving as many parts as possible. Their gun was indexed ZIK-1 and was theoretically compatible with both the KV-1 and T-34. The design remained on paper, but work on similar weapons continued. By the spring of 1943 factory #9 (an organization dedicated to the development of tank guns split out of factory #8) had another 85 mm gun in the works.[124] This gun was initially called D-7, but in May of 1943 it was renamed D-5T-85[125] (later just D-5T).[126] This gun traces its roots back to the U-12 gun. Unlike the S-31, the D-5T-85 did not reuse any existing parts, but it was more compact than its competitor and had a less vulnerable mantlet design. Even though this went against the army's requirements, chief designer at factory #9 F.F. Petrov felt that this gamble would pay off.[127]

New Prototypes and Trials

Factory #100 was instructed to build two prototype tanks, one with the TsAKB's (Central Artillery Design Bureau) S-31 and one with factory

---

[123] Y. Pasholok, *Bolshaya Pushka dlya Nebolshoy Bashni*, https://warspot.ru/8778-bolshaya-pushka-dlya-nebolshoy-bashni, retrieved on May 15th, 2021

[124] TsAMO RF F.81 Op.12063 D.19 L.15-16

[125] The letter D in the designation indicates that the gun was designed at factory #9 in Sverdlovsk.

[126] TsAMO RF F.81 Op.12063 D.19 L.155-156

[127] Y. Pasholok, *Ot Srednego Shturmovika k Srednemu Istrebitelyu*, https://warspot.ru/10662-put-ot-srednego-shturmovika-k-srednemu-istrebitelyu, retrieved on May 16th, 2021

#9's D-5T-85.[128] The new tank was given the blueprint index 237 and a new name: IS-3. It took two months to implement all the required changes and complete the assembly of a chassis. Around this time the factory began referring to its design projects using the designation "Object", and so the IS-3 became Object 237.[129] By this time there were already four S-31 guns and one D-5T-85 delivered to factory #100. The single D-5T-85 was reserved for Object 239 (future KV-85), and so both Object 237 prototypes ended up equipped with S-31 guns.

The first mobility trials began at the end of May.[130] These trials showed that the decision to add a sixth road wheel and expand the tank was correct. There were some deviations from the requirements, for instance the use of the 520 hp V-2-IS engine rather than the 600 hp V-2K. The new tank weighed 43 tons, lower than expected, and so even the weaker engine provided satisfactory mobility. More importantly, there were no signs of overheating even in hot summer weather. The new Multicyclone air filter also worked effectively.[131]

The tanks were supposed to be submitted for full trials by July 1st with a conclusion provided by July 10th, but this didn't happen on time.[132] Production delays meant that trials of the two 85 mm guns were delayed until August of 1943, but by then they were only a formality. A battle between the two design bureaus already took place at the trials of SU-85 prototypes held in July of 1943.[133] Factory #9 presented the D-5S-85 gun (formerly D-5) against the TsAKB's (Central Artillery Design Bureau) S-18, the SPG variant of the S-31. The D-5S-85 demonstrated a shorter recoil length, higher rate of fire, and fewer issues with the

[128] TsAMO RF F.38 Op.11355 D.1529 L.13-15
[129] TsAMO RF F.38 Op.11355 D.1377 L.195
[130] TsAMO RF F.38 Op.11355 D.1634 L.7-8
[131] Y. Pasholok, *IS Kotoriy Poluchilsya*, https://warspot.ru/10487-is-kotoryy-poluchilsya, retrieved on May 16th, 2021
[132] A.M. Radionov and others, *Glavnoye Bronetankovoye Upravleniye: lyudi, sobytia, fakty v dokumentakh 1943-1944 gg kniga III*, Ministry of Defense of the Russian Federation, Moscow, 2006. p.268
[133] TsAMO RF F.38 Op.11369 D.107 L.7-8

recoil system. While neither gun was perfect, the winner was clear.[134] Stalin signed GKO (State Committee of Defense) decree #3892ss on August 8th, 1943, putting the D-5S-85 into service.[135]

The KV-85

A similar contest was fought on the tank front. The TsAKB (Central Artillery Design Bureau) presented the S-31 gun for installation into the stock KV-1S turret, factory #9's D-5T-85 gun was installed in the turret of the Object 239 tank, a KV-1S hull with a widened turret ring and a turret from the Object 237.[136] The result was the same as with the SPGs. The recoil length of the D-5T-85 was lower and the larger turret allowed for a much higher rate of fire: 10-13 RPM.[137] Stalin accepted the Object 239 into service as the KV-85 in GKO (State Committee of Defense) decree #3891ss signed on August 8th. 22 of these vehicles were now due in August, 63 in September of 1943. The August quota for KV-1S tanks and SU-152 SPGs was lowered to 21 and 84 units respectively.[138]

Final Trials

Even though the results were predictable, trials of the two kinds of Object 237 tanks were still held at the Gorohovets proving grounds between August 22nd and August 24th, 1943.[139] The D-5T-85 gun proved its superiority once again. The trials showed that it had higher

[134] Y. Pasholok, *Ot Srednego Shturmovika k Srednemu Istrebitelyu*, https://warspot.ru/10662-put-ot-srednego-shturmovika-k-srednemu-istrebitelyu, retrieved on May 16th, 2021
[135] RGASPI F.644 Op.2 D.202 L.139-148
[136] TsAMO RF F.38 Op.11355 D.1529 L.13-15
[137] Y. Pasholok, *Kutsak Kotina*, https://warspot.ru/10800-kutsak-kotina, retrieved on May 16th, 2021
[138] RGASPI F.644 Op.2 D.202 L.135-138
[139] TsAMO RF F.38 Op.11355 D.1529 L.13-15

precision than the S-31 due to a better recoil system, higher rate of fire (up to 15 RPM), smaller dimensions, greater reliability, and better balance, which made counterweights unnecessary. The recoil mechanism was improved and no longer malfunctioned.[140] The smaller breech and shorter recoil allowed for greater gun depression (-3.5° vs -2°) and elevation (22° vs 21°). This also meant that the dead zone in front of the tank was smaller (23 m vs 50 m).[141] Stalin signed GKO (State Committee of Defense) decree #4043ss on September 4th, 1943, accepting the Object 237 with the 85 mm D-5T-85 gun into service under the name IS.[142]

Production

The decree allotted plenty of time for production to be set up. The first 25 vehicles were due in November of 1943, then 75 tanks in December. To free up resources, production of the KV-85 would cease in October with 63 vehicles delivered that month, SU-152 production would cease in November with 42 vehicles delivered.[143] The SU-152 SPG would be replaced with the ISU-152 on the chassis of the new heavy tank. 5 of these vehicles were due in November and 30 in December. The quota for T-34 tanks was not relaxed, in fact it was increased from 335 to 350 units monthly starting with October of 1943.[144] This way the tank was entering production in two stages: the turret entered production in August and the first hulls would be assembled in November. One of the biggest issues with starting up production was the casting, particularly the hull. Until then, the hulls of Soviet tanks were either built from bent rolled plates welded together (KV-1)[145] or flat rolled plates welded to

---

[140] TsAMO RF F.38 Op.11355 D.1529 L.13-15

[141] TsAMO RF F.38 Op.11355 D.1529 L.3

[142] RGASPI F.644 Op.2 D.211 L.1

[143] A.G. Solyankin and others, Sovietskiye Tyazheliye Samokhodniye Artilleriyskiye Ustanovki 1941-1945, Tseyghaus, Moscow, 2006, pp.6-7

[144] RGASPI F.644 Op.2 D.211 L.2

[145] M. Kolomiyets, *Leningradskiye KV*, Tactical Press, Moscow, 2013. pp.112-113

small cast components (T-34)[146]. Experiments with cast hulls performed in 1941 ended in failures, but ones Soviet tank designers could learn from.[147] Now the hull of the IS-2 was almost entirely composed of large cast components. There were also several design issues identified during trials that would have to be corrected before production began. For instance, the exhaust system had to be modified to prevent the fumes from being sucked back into the cooling system. The driver's observation port was changed to improve his vision. The trials commission also considered the 520 hp engine insufficient and required a 600 hp engine to be installed, but this change was postponed. 19 change requests in total were reviewed at a meeting held on September 13th, 2 of which were to be put into production immediately and 12 more by December 1st. The postponed changes included new track links. Different designs made from different steels were tested on the Object 237 from November 20th to 30th.[148]

The first two IS tanks were assembled at the Kirov factory ahead of schedule, in late October of 1943. This tempo was hard to keep up; even though the first November production tank was delivered by November 5th only three tanks were delivered by November 16th and the final tank from the November batch was only delivered on the morning of December 1st. Only 14 out of 25 tanks passed quality control. It turned out that only the workers that were involved in assembly of the Object 237 tanks and were familiar with the new design assembled high quality IS tanks, the others made mistakes due to faulty documentation. There were also plenty of design issues that were only discovered in production tanks. Delays were also caused due to slower than expected hull and turret production at factory #200.[149]

[146] P. Samsonov, *Designing the T-34*, Gallantry Books, Horncastle, 2019, p.58

[147] M. Kolomiyets, *Leningradskiye KV*, Tactical Press, Moscow, 2013. p.97

[148] Y. Pasholok, *Promezhutochniy IS*, https://warspot.ru/11074-promezhutochnyy-is, retrieved on May 22nd, 2021

[149] Y. Pasholok, *Promezhutochniy IS*, https://warspot.ru/11074-promezhutochnyy-is, retrieved on May 22nd, 2021

The IS tank was considered a temporary measure from the very start. Decree #4043ss that accepted it into service already called for the production of a tank with a 122 mm gun, and so quotas for the IS inevitably decreased to free up resources for the newcomer. With the appearance of the second IS tank, the name of the first was retroactively changed. Various period sources refer to it as "IS-1", "IS-85",[150] and "IS tank with an 85 mm gun",[151] although official documents including monthly production plans continued to call it simply "IS" even after its successor had entered production.[152] The quota for December was lowered to 40 tanks. 40 more tanks were built in January of 1944 for a total of 107 IS tanks produced. Not a single vehicle of this type survives to this day.[153]

---

[150] TsAMO RF F.307 Op.4148 D.1 L.99
[151] RGASPI F.644 Op.2 D.211 L.10
[152] RGASPI F.644 Op.1 D.182 L.248
[153] Y. Pasholok, *Promezhutochniy IS*, https://warspot.ru/11074-promezhutochnyy-is, retrieved on May 22nd, 2021

A Futureproof Gun

While the 85 mm 52-K gun and tank guns with the same ballistics turned out to be effective weapons against the Tiger tank,[154] the wartime arms race between guns and armor continued at a breakneck pace. New opponents arose by the time the IS tank with an 85 mm gun was accepted into service: the Panther tank and Ferdinand tank destroyer. Samples of both vehicles were captured at the Battle of Kursk. Trials carried out at the NIBT Proving Grounds showed that the 85 mm gun was no longer enough. The Panther's upper front hull plate was 80 mm thick and placed at an angle of 35 degrees from horizontal. This armor could not be penetrated by the 85 mm 52-K gun even at a range of 100 meters.[155] The Ferdinand tank destroyer had up to 200 mm of front armor. No attempt to fire on it was even made during trials, the 85 mm gun was only fired against the side.[156] Work on an 85 mm gun with a muzzle velocity increased to 1000 m/s began to deal with these vehicles, but development would take some time. Using a higher caliber gun with proven ballistics was a faster option. Such a gun was available: the 122 mm model 1931 corps gun (A-19[157]). This was a high-power field artillery weapon designed to combat powerful fortifications from a range of up to 20 kilometers.[158] Its high muzzle velocity and large caliber made it a potent weapon for a next generation heavy tank.

---

[154] Tsamo RF F.38 Op.11377 D.12 L.33

[155] Y. Pasholok, *Strashnee Koshki Zverya Net*, https://warspot.ru/11907-strashnee-koshki-zverya-net, retrieved on December 15th, 2021

[156] Y. Pasholok, *Tyazheliy Trofey s Kurskoy Dugi*, https://warspot.ru/10672-tyazhyolyy-trofey-s-kurskoy-dugi, retrieved on December 15th, 2021

[157] The letter A in the designation indicates that the gun was designed at experimental artillery factory #38 in Podlipki, Moscow oblast (modern day Korolev). Not to be confused with designs produced at tank factory #183 which also used the letter A in its project designations.

[158] A. Mernikov, *Vooruzhenniye Sily SSSR i Germanii 1939-1945*, Harvest, Minsk, 2010, p.88

122 mm model 1931 corps gun (A-19). This powerful gun laid the foundation for the D-25T gun used in the IS-2 tank. Canadian War Museum, Rifled breech loading gun, CWM 19660016-007. *(Peter Samsonov)*

Putting an Artillery Gun into a Turret

Trials held in May of 1941 showed that the A-19 could penetrate 100 mm thick armor positioned at a 30 degree angle at 1000 meters with its G-471[159] concrete piercing shell, making it a potent weapon against potential German heavy tanks.[160] When such a tank finally appeared, the Red Army was ready. The A-19 gun took part in the aforementioned penetration trials of a Tiger tank held in April of 1943. The A-19 demonstrated great effectiveness: the first shot went through an existing opening in the front of the hull and penetrated the rear plate

---

[159] The letter G in an ammunition code indicates a concrete piercing shell.
[160] TsAMO RF F.38 Op.12104 D.261 L.7

from 1500 meters. The second shot penetrated the turret at 1500 meters, tore off a large section of the armor, dislodged the turret from the turret ring, and pushed it back by 540 mm. This gun turned out to be an effective weapon against the new German tank.[161]

Factory #9 began working on a 122 mm tank gun with the ballistics of the A-19 in May of 1943. As with the 85 mm tank guns, there was no need to start from scratch. Work on a lightened version of the A-19 gun installed on an M-30 howitzer carriage began back in October of 1942. The barrel was shortened from 5620 to 5520 mm and a double baffle muzzle brake was used to protect the lighter carriage from the recoil.[162] This work had even reached the practical stage: construction of a prototype was authorized in February of 1943. A draft project for the installation of this yet unnamed gun in the turret of an IS tank was ready by July 14th. The weapon combined features from existing designs: the cradle of the D-5 gun, the breech of the A-19, and the barrel of an experimental D-2 122 mm gun. Ammunition was also taken from the A-19.[163]

This gun weighed 900 kg more than the 85 mm D-5T-85, but a new T-shaped muzzle brake gave it a recoil length of just 550 mm, making it suitable for installation into the existing turret.[164] This project received official approval and a name on September 4th. Decree #4043ss referred to it as D-25, a portmanteau of D-2 and D-5.[165] A tank with this gun was due on October 1st.[166] The first D-25 gun was completed in metal on September 15th and went through trials that lasted from September 16th to the 23rd. The gun passed trials, but the muzzle brake

[161] TsAMO RF F.38 Op.11377 D.12 L.37
[162] TsAMO RF F.38 Op.11355 D.1702 L.3
[163] Y. Pasholok, *Is s Tyazhelym Vooruzheniyev*, https://warspot.ru/11233-is-s-tyazhyolym-vooruzheniem , retrieved on May 22nd, 2021
[164] Y. Pasholok, *Is s Tyazhelym Vooruzheniyev*, https://warspot.ru/11233-is-s-tyazhyolym-vooruzheniem , retrieved on May 22nd, 2021
[165] M. Baryatinskiy, Tyazheliy tank IS-2, Yauza, Moscow, 2006, p.16
[166] RGASPI F.644 Op.2 D.211 L.1

deformed during firing.[167] As time was of the essence, the gun was shipped from factory #9 to ChKZ (Kirov Factory in Chelyabinsk) as-is on September 25th as work on a new muzzle brake was still underway. The solution to this problem had German roots. Inspiration was taken from the muzzle brake of the 8.8 cm Pak 43 gun installed on a captured Ferdinand SPG. This fact was not concealed and this muzzle brake design was even openly called "Ferdinand style" in Soviet documents.[168]

4th serial production IS-2 tank (serial number 1223124) with a "Ferdinand" style muzzle brake, Chelyabinsk Kirov Factory. Note the T-34 tanks in the background. The factory was required to produce them in parallel with heavy tanks until March 1944.

The new tank received blueprint index 240 at ChKZ (Kirov Factory in Chelyabinsk) and the designation Object 240.[169] Object 240 was not built from scratch. The chassis of the second Object 237 was taken as the basis. The D-25 gun was installed in the tank on September 30th. Some changes were required as a result of the installation. The rear

---

[167] M. Baryatinskiy, Tyazheliy tank IS-2, Yauza, Moscow, 2006, p.16
[168] TsAMO RF F.81 Op.12038 D.313 L.106
[169] TsAMO RF F.38 Op.11355 D.2571 L.60

machine gun was removed from the prototype to make room for the radio, although its mount remained.[170] In order to make more room for the larger gun, the slope of the front section of the roof was reduced from 5 to 3 degrees.[171] A more powerful extractor fan was installed. The ammunition racks were replaced and now held only 28 rounds. The tank's weight increased to an estimated 45.5-46 tons, and the top speed was expected to decrease to 32.5 kph. Brief trials followed. The tank drove to the factory shooting range where it nearly caused a tragedy. The old muzzle brake burst during firing and its fragments nearly struck Piotr Voroshilov, Kliment Voroshilov's adopted son.[172]

[170] A.G. Solyankin and others, *Sovetskiye tyazheliye tanki 1941-1945*, Tseyghaus, Moscow, 2007, p.103

[171] A.G. Solyankin and others, *Sovetskiye tyazheliye tanki 1941-1945*, Tseyghaus, Moscow, 2007, p.59

[172] Y. Pasholok, *Is s Tyazhelym Vooruzheniyev*, https://warspot.ru/11233-is-s-tyazhyolym-vooruzheniem, retrieved on May 22nd, 2021

Mobility and Gunnery Trials

Mobility trials began on the next day and lasted until October 4th. The tank drove from Chelyabinsk to Zlatoust and back, a distance of 345 km (178 of which was on a highway). Performance of the Object 240 was compared to that of an Object 237 tank, which also took part in the trials. The average movement speed decreased due to the added weight: Object 240 gave a speed of 18.1 kph while the Object 237 was slightly faster at 21.5 kph. Object 237 got stuck twice and Object 240 had to be used to pull it out. The tank proved more than capable at towing its lighter cousin. A second stage of trials began on October 6th. The tanks drove from Chelyabinsk to Sineglazovo and back. 10 km of this route took place on paved roads, 20 km on dirt roads, and 81 km off-road. This time the average speed of the two tanks was the same. Fears about a radical decrease in mobility as a result of a heavier gun proved baseless. Trials continued and Object 240 drove for a total of 1263 km (714 on a highway, 468 on dirt roads, and 81 off-road) in October in addition to the 355 km the chassis drove before conversion.[173]

The prototype arrived at the Gorohovets Scientific Research Artillery Proving Grounds (GANIOP) to take part in gunnery trials on October 18th, 1943. The new muzzle brake arrived the next day. The muzzle velocity of AP and HE shells was measured as 2.2-2.65% lower than the muzzle velocity of the A-19. Two factors contributed to this: the barrel of the D-2 was slightly shorter than that of the A-19, and the gun had already fired 172 rounds before it was installed in the tank. The muzzle velocity dropped 1% between the start and end of the trials due to barrel wear, which was considered acceptable. In total, the experimental D-25 gun made 474 shots: 214 supercharged, 213 with the full propellant charge, and 47 with a reduced charge. The muzzle brake cracked during trials, but did not burst like the first design. Precision of

[173] Y. Pasholok, *Is s Tyazhelym Vooruzheniyev*, https://warspot.ru/11233-is-s-tyazhyolym-vooruzheniem , retrieved on May 22nd, 2021

the gun was high, on par with the precision of the A-19.[174] See the section titled *Precision of the D-25T* for more details.

Ergonomics

An ergonomics study of the Object 240 was also conducted. The loader's workspace was criticized the harshest. The new tank had the same turret dimensions as the Object 237, but the D-25T gun breech was larger than the D-5T, reducing the amount of space he had to work. Its width was now 680 mm, fairly narrow, but still possible to perform his duties. The distance between the recoil guard and turret ring was now just 200 mm, making it impossible to go around the gun to get to the other side of the turret; the only route was underneath it. The fighting compartment was also not tall enough at 1600 mm and a loader of average height had to slouch when standing. Both the floor racks and the ready rack in the turret bustle were criticized. The loading assistance device was a double-edged sword: it helped the loader handle the bulky ammunition, but also reduced the amount of space available to him. The screw breech also confined the loader's movements when opened, so the commander had to assist him in this process. Because of these impediments, the rate of fire was rather low at 2-3 RPM.[175]

The gunner's workspace was also narrower than on the Object 240's predecessor, now 650 mm. The height of the fighting compartment was less important for him, as he worked in a sitting position. There were still plenty of criticisms to go around. For instance, the commission criticized the elevation of the gun. It took 5-10 kg of effort to elevate it and 1-5 kg to depress it. The maximum gun depression was -3 degrees, the maximum elevation was +24 degrees 30 minutes. It took 24 ¾ rotations of the flywheel or 7 seconds to cover this entire range. Rotation of the

---

[174] Y. Pasholok, *Is s Tyazhelym Vooruzheniyev*, https://warspot.ru/11233-is-s-tyazhyolym-vooruzheniem , retrieved on May 22nd, 2021
[175] TsAMO RF F.38 Op.11355 D.1525 L.37-39

turret was more difficult: it took 3-25 kg of effort to turn the flywheel, and 974 turns or 570 seconds to traverse 360 degrees by hand. The commission required for the traverse rate to be faster and the effort applied to be even.[176]

The ventilation of the fighting compartment was found to be sufficient. Firing with the hatches closed, ventilation fan on, and engine running could be sustained indefinitely without danger to the crew. Firing with the hatches closed, engine off, and fan off could still be performed for a short amount of time.[177]

The drawbacks revealed in trials of the Object 240 were relatively minor and were corrected before it went into production. On October 31st, 1943, Stalin signed GKO (State Committee of Defense, *Gosudarstvenniy Komitet Oborony*) decree #4479ss accepting the tank into production. Assembly was expected to begin in November.[178]

Decree #4479ss gave the tank a new name: IS-2.[179] Its predecessor was retroactively renamed IS-1, reusing the indices of the tanks with blueprint indices 234 and 233. This would not be the last time that a production IS series tank reclaimed the index used by a prototype. The new vehicles were also referred to as "IS tank with an 85 mm gun" and "IS tank with a 122 mm gun" or IS-85 and IS-122 for short.[180]

---

[176] TsAMO RF F.38 Op.11355 D.1525 L.38
[177] TsAMO RF F.38 Op.11355 D.1525 L.41
[178] RGASPI F.644 Op.2 D.239 L.101
[179] RGASPI F.644 Op.2 D.239 L.101
[180] TsAMO RF F.38 Op.11355 D.3012 L.102-105

Penetration Trials

The decision to begin installation of 122 mm guns was proven correct in penetration trials that began on December 1st at the NIBT Proving Grounds. It turned out that the 85 mm D-5 gun could not penetrate the upper front plate of a Panther tank at even 100 meters. Its shells had a tendency to ricochet. The 122 mm D-25T on the other hand penetrated the upper front plate on the first shot from a range of 1400 meters.[181] The power of the gun was also demonstrated when firing at the side of the tank: a shell penetrated the left side of the turret, went straight through, and tore off the right side entirely. The D-25 gun could reliably penetrate any part of the Panther's armor at a range of up to 2000 meters, while the D-5 could only penetrate the gun mantlet and the front of the turret at that range.[182]

Penetration trials held against a captured Ferdinand at the NIBT Proving Grounds around this time confirmed these findings. The 85 mm D-5 had no hope of penetrating the front armor, but was guaranteed to penetrate the side of the hull and casemate at a range of 900 meters.[183] The 122 mm D-25 performed much better, with a penetration of the casemate front at a range of 1400 meters.[184] The shell was lodged in the armor, but the fragments that were dislodged would have killed the crew and disabled the vehicle anyway. Soviet testers estimated that the D-25 would be guaranteed to penetrate the front armor at 1000 meters.[185]

---

[181] Y. Pasholok, *Strashnee koshki zverya net*, https://warspot.ru/11907-strashnee-koshki-zverya-net, retrieved on May 24th, 2021

[182] TsAMO RF F.38 Op.11355 D.2375 L.2

[183] Y. Bakhurin, *Panzerjager Tiger (P) Ferdinand*, Tactical Press, Moscow, 2014, p.69

[184] Y. Bakhurin, *Panzerjager Tiger (P) Ferdinand*, Tactical Press, Moscow, 2014, p.70-71

[185] Y. Pasholok, *Tyazheliy trofey s Kurskoy dugi*, https://warspot.ru/10672-tyazhyolyy-trofey-s-kurskoy-dugi, retrieved on May 24th, 2021

Penetration Tests Against the Königstiger and Maus

The IS-2's powerful gun came in handy a year later, when the Red Army first encountered Tiger II tanks with even more effective frontal armor than the Panther or Ferdinand. Trials held in October of 1944 showed that the A-19 (and thus the D-25) was still effective against this tank. The first shot fired was an HE shell from 100 meters. The shell struck the upper front plate below the machine gun ball. The shockwave resulted in cracked weld seams around the machine gun mount and burst bolts holding it on. The weld seam between the right side and upper front plate also burst and the side plate was bent outward by 5 mm. Flames entered the tank through the new opening and caused a small fire. The tank would have been disabled by this attack.[186] Shot #2 (blunt-tipped AP at impact velocity matching 2700 m) ricocheted. Shot #3 (blunt-tipped AP from 500 m) failed to penetrate the armor, but still dealt catastrophic damage. The weld seam between the upper front plate and the hull roof burst completely, as did the seam between the upper and lower front plates and the seam between the left pannier floor and left side. A 160 by 170 mm fragment of the armor 50 mm thick was dislodged on the inside. The driver's observation device was knocked off. This attack would also have destroyed the German tank.[187] The next shot fired a sharp-tipped AP shell from 600 meters. This hit resulted in a complete penetration, dislodging a 580 by 500 mm fragment of armor 80 mm thick on the inside. This penetration was not counted as satisfactory, since it was too close to the impact made by shot #3. Shot #5 (sharp-tipped AP from 700 m) did not penetrate the armor, but a 150 mm long crack formed in the plate with more weld seams destroyed.[188] The next shot fired by the A-19 was made at a range of 2500 m with blunt tipped AP and aimed at the lower front plate.

---

[186] TsAMO RF F.38 Op.11377 D.129 L.11
[187] TsAMO RF F.38 Op.11377 D.129 L.13-14
[188] TsAMO RF F.38 Op.11377 D.129 L.15

Penetration was not achieved, and only more cracked weld seams were recorded.[189]

Testers then switched to other guns, but this was not the last attack the A-19 made. Shot #32 was made with a 122 mm sharp-tipped AP shell at a range of 500 meters. The hit landed on the upper part of the upper front plate. The upper front plate caved in.[190]

The trials shifted to the turret. Sharp-tipped AP fired from 2400 m hit near an existing penetration and was thus not counted, but the results were still spectacular. A 250 by 300 mm fragment of armor 80 mm thick was knocked off from the front of the turret and a 300 by 600 mm breach formed in the back. A 400 by 700 mm portion of the roof broke off. The weld seam between the side of the turret and the roof burst along a length of 800 mm.[191]

A second shot from 122 mm shape-tipped AP to the front of the tank from 2500 m was counted as satisfactory. The shell made a 700 by 220 mm breach in the front armor and 460 by 300 mm breach in the roof, forming two cracks over a meter long.[192] The final shot was fired at 3400 m with blunt-tipped AP. It did not penetrate the front turret armor, although there was a new crack found in a weld seam.[193] The testers concluded that the A-19 gun is capable of penetrating the front turret armor of a Tiger II tank from 1000-1500 meters and the upper front plate at 500-600 meters on a favorable hit. Even nonpenetrating hits from AP or HE shells resulted in destruction of the armor and damage to weld seams.[194]

---

[189] TsAMO RF F.38 Op.11377 D.129 L.16
[190] TsAMO RF F.38 Op.11377 D.129 L.35
[191] TsAMO RF F.38 Op.11377 D.129 L.35
[192] TsAMO RF F.38 Op.11377 D.129 L.36-37
[193] TsAMO RF F.38 Op.11377 D.129 L.38
[194] TsAMO RF F.38 Op.11377 D.129 L.2

The effectiveness of the D-25 gun was also evaluated against the Maus tank prototype in 1946. Based on a combination of practical trials and investigation of the armor composition made by Soviet scientists, the 122 mm AP shell was expected to penetrate[195] the 185 mm thick vertical side at velocities greater than 700 m/s, the 160 mm thick upper rear plate sloped at 35 degrees at 740 m/s, and the 160 mm thick lower rear plate sloped at 30 degrees at 700 m/s.[196] This corresponds to approximately 1200 m and 500 m respectively when using the blunt-tipped BR[197]-471B shell or 800 m and 400 m when using the sharp-tipped BR-471 shell fired from the D-25 gun.[198] Penetrating the front armor of the German superheavy tank was out of the question for the D-25. The weakest portion of the frontal armor, the vertical area of the turret front, could be penetrated at a velocity of 830 m/s, higher than the D-25's muzzle velocity of 781 m/s. The lower front plate was an even tougher target with a penetration limit of 925 m/s, and the upper front hull armor was the most difficult to penetrate with a critical velocity of 1300 m/s.[199] It is interesting to note that the BL-9, BL-13-1, and S-26-1 experimental 122 mm guns designed for installation in IS tanks and ISU SPGs that were built and tested in the USSR in 1944-1945 had a muzzle velocity of 1000 m/s, meaning that they would have been able to engage the Maus frontally.[200]

---

[195] The limit of complete penetration (predel skvoznogo probitiya) metric was used in these evaluations. The number indicates the minimum velocity at which the shell or its fragments pass through the armor plate of the given thickness after penetration.

[196] Vestnik Bronetankovoy Promyshlennosti #5-6, Mintransmash, Moscow, 1946, p.26

[197] BR: broneboyniy, armor piercing

[198] Tablitsi strelby 122-mm tankovoy pushki obr. 1943g (D-25T) TS #144T 7th edition, Publisher of the Ministry of Defense of the USSR, Moscow, 1969

[199] Vestnik Bronetankovoy Promyshlennosti #5-6, Mintransmash, Moscow, 1946, p.26

[200] TsAMO RF F.38 Op.11369 D.696 L.190

Precision of the D-25T

The D-25T gun was not just powerful, but it was also precise. Gunnery was a common aspect of warranty trials, and the guns' precision was measured in the process. At a range of 1000 meters a grouping of 10 shells fell into a circle with a radius of 70-90 cm with the best 50% of the shots hitting within a 24-40 cm circle. At 2000 meters the groupings were 120-130 cm in diameter with the best 50% falling within 45-90 cm of the mean point of impact. This degree of precision allowed the IS-2 tank to hit a tank-sized target at a considerable distance.[201] We can compare these results with trials of the 85 mm ZIS-S-53 gun in a prototype of the T-44 tank. After being broken in, the best 50% of the shots landed in a circle with a radius of 36 cm and the radius of the whole group was 54 cm.[202]

The performance of the 122 mm D-25T gun was comparable to that of the tank's most dangerous enemy, the Tiger II. In Soviet trials, the tank's 8.8 cm KwK 43 gun made a 50% groupings of 36-43 cm and 100% groupings of 48-67 cm at 1000 meters. At 2000 meters, the groupings were 62 and 93 cm in diameter respectively, making the performance of these two guns quite similar.[203]

Unfortunately, since different nations collected precision data in different ways (for instance, the British measured 90% zones[204]), direct comparisons with guns only tested outside of the USSR is difficult.

Based on the results of these trials, one can conclusively say that the D-25 gun remained a viable weapon against any tank the IS-2 faced or

---

[201] TsAMO RF F.38 Op.11355 D.2380 L.8, TsAMO RF F.38 Op.11355 D.2349 L.22, TsAMO RF F.38 Op.11355 D.2852 L.15, TsAMO RF F.38 Op.11355 D.2855 L.27-28

[202] Andrey Tarasenko, *Poligonniye ispytaniya vtorogo opytnogo obraztsa tanka T-44 konstruktsii zavoda #183 NKTP*, http://btvt.info/1inservice/t-44-1944-tests.htm, retrieved on July 21st, 2022

[203] TsAMO RF F.38 Op.11355 D.2860 L.18

[204] Canadian Military Headquarters, London (CMHQ), Files Block No. 55 – reel 5776, image 2713

could have conceivably faced during the Second World War. It is not surprising that this gun remained the weapon of choice for Soviet heavy tanks for over a decade.[205]

Silhouette of a Tiger tank with the D-25T gun's maximum dispersion zones at 1000 meters (70-90 cm) and 2000 meters (120-130 cm) overlaid. If aiming at the center of mass, all of the IS-2's shots would hit a tank-sized target at any realistic range for a Second World War era tank duel. *(Peter Samsonov)*

[205] Y. Pasholok, *Posledniy sovetskiy tyazheloves*, https://warspot.ru/4474-posledniy-sovetskiy-tyazheloves, retrieved on May 24th, 2021

Metamorphosis and Mass Production

As mentioned above, assembly of IS-2 tanks was expected to begin on November 20th. 10 units were due between then and the end of the month, 15 more in the first half of December, 20 in the second half, and 75 units in January of 1944.[206] Transition from the KV-1S to the IS-1 also affected vehicles on the KV-1S chassis. The SU-152 SPG was replaced with the ISU-152, an equivalent vehicle on the IS-1 chassis, which also entered production in November of 1943. 5 units were due that month and 30 more in December. ChKZ (Kirov Factory in Chelyabinsk) was also expected to deliver 350 T-34 tanks per month.[207] Production of new heavy tanks and SPGs was a difficult task, and so the quota was quickly relaxed. On December 27th, 1943, Stalin signed GKO (State Committee of Defense) decree #4850ss, lowering the requirement for T-34 tank production to 150 units monthly. Quotas for heavy vehicles were increased instead: 125 units in January (40 IS-1, 35 IS-2, 50 ISU-152), 150 in February (75 IS-2 and 75 ISU-152), 250 in March (100 IS-2 and 150 ISU-152), and 300 units per month starting in April (150 each).[208] See Table 1 for a full list of production quotas.

Improvements During Production

As with many vehicles entering production, the tank started changing almost immediately. A new turret was introduced on January 19th, 1944. The gun mantlet was widened and the gun sight opening was moved to the left. The shape of the commander's cupola bulge changed to make the turret easier to cast. These turrets were first installed starting in February of 1944, and completely replaced old turrets in March. New turret "cheeks" were also developed at the same time, but were not introduced into production until the summer of 1944.

---

[206] RGASPI F.644 Op.2 D.239 L.101
[207] RGASPI F.644 Op.2 D.211 L.2
[208] RGASPI F.644 Op.2 D.254 L.127-128

The Ural Heavy Machinebuilding Factory (UZTM) joined factory #200 as a producer of IS-2 hulls and turrets in January of 1944. These components entered production at ChKZ (Kirov Factory in Chelyabinsk) in February. Components produced at UZTM were visually different[209]: the front hull casting produced at factory #200 had a casting number on the left side and bulges on the lower front armor. UZTM hulls had a casting mark at the joint between the upper and lower front armor and no casting number. A similar difference can be seen in the turret: factory #200 had a casting number in the rear, UZTM ones did not. The turrets can also be distinguished by the shape of the commander's cupola and the casting seam. Factory #178 also joined as a subcontractor, delivering commander's cupolas. As Mariupol was liberated in September of 1943, the Mariupol Ilyich factory was rebuilt and began producing armor once more. Even though supplies were limited, the quality of Mariupol's products was deemed higher than that of factory #200. Mariupol turrets were similar to those produced at UZTM, but they had a casting number in the rear.[210] Hammer and Sickle factory in Moscow also joined in, producing turrets starting in May of 1944. Hammer and Sickle turrets had no casting numbers, but they had reinforcement ribs around the rear machine gun ball mount and a straight casting seam that ran along the lower part of the turret. The texture of the turrets was also rougher. Deliveries from Moscow paled in comparison to the other manufacturers, with only 103 turrets delivered in 1944 compared to Mariupol's 922.[211]

[209] M. Baryatinskiy, Tyazheliy tank IS-2, Yauza, Moscow, 2006, p.33-34
[210] Y. Pasholok, *Borba za mesto na konveyere*, https://warspot.ru/11457-borba-za-mesto-na-konveyere, retrieved on May 27th, 2021
[211] Y. Pasholok, *Malaya modernizatsiya bolshogo tanka*, https://warspot.ru/12831-malaya-modernizatsiya-bolshogo-tanka, retrieved on May 30th, 2021

IS-2M tank installed at 10 Tamansyaka St, Moscow. The turret was originally produced at Mariupol, the hull at factory #200. (*Nikita Trutnev*)

IS-2 tank in Nizhnekamsk. The turret was produced at the Hammer and Sickle factory in Moscow, the hull was produced at UZTM. (*Nikita Trutnev*)

Improving the Rate of Fire

Work was also done on the gun. One of the tank's most obvious weaknesses was the low rate of fire. A meeting was held at factory #9 on November 22nd, 1943, to try and find ways to mitigate this drawback.[212] One solution was to replace the screw breech with a semiautomatic sliding one. Two variants were developed: one with a horizontal breech and one with a vertical one opening to the left.[213] The latter was selected for production in metal. Two prototypes were finished by January 1st, 1944, and sent for trials on January 4th. These guns had another novelty: a new muzzle brake. Trials showed that the rate of fire indeed increased, but the muzzle brake failed trials again. A new design was quickly developed, dubbed "#7 extra reinforced". This muzzle brake was tested between January 3rd and 16th over the course of 300 shots. A gun with the new muzzle brake was sent to factory #100 on January 24th, and as it was obviously superior to the old type, production of the D-25T gun with a new muzzle brake and semiautomatic breech began in February of 1944.[214]

---

[212] Y. Pasholok, *Borba za mesto na konveyere*, https://warspot.ru/11457-borba-za-mesto-na-konveyere, retrieved on May 27th, 2021
[213] TsAMO RF F.81 Op.12038 D.188 L.84
[214] M. Baryatinskiy, *Tyazheliy tank IS-2*, Yauza, Moscow, 2006, p.17

This style of muzzle brake was used as of February of 1944. It replaced the "Ferdinand style" muzzle brake. Guns with these muzzle brakes also had semi-automatic breeches. Patriot Park. (*Pavel Borovikov*)

An experimental tank with the new gun entered trials at the Kopeisk proving grounds on February 11th. 50 shots were made over the course of three days. The new breech was smaller and lighter. The loader now had more room to work, but a 60 kg counterweight was required to keep the gun in balance. The experimental tank also had the new TSh-17 gun sight.[215] Trials showed that the rate of fire improved by one round per minute compared to the initial design of the gun, and so the improved D-25T gun with a new breech and muzzle brake entered production in the beginning of March of 1944.[216] 145 IS-2 tanks were produced with the old screw breech and "Ferdinand style" muzzle brake.[217]

[215] M. Baryatinskiy, Tyazheliy tank IS-2, Yauza, Moscow, 2006, p.17
[216] M. Baryatinskiy, Tyazheliy tank IS-2, Yauza, Moscow, 2006, p.19
[217] Y. Pasholok, *Borba za mesto na konveyere*, https://warspot.ru/11457-borba-za-mesto-na-konveyere, retrieved on May 27th, 2021

The introduction of the new gun coincided with some other changes. The TSh-17 sight required a new wider gun mantlet. During the transitional period gun mantlets were produced with two openings, one for the TSh-17 and one for the older 10T-17.[218] The PT4-17 periscopic sight was also replaced with the MK-4 periscope around this time.[219]

March also marked another revision to production quotas. ChKZ (Kirov Factory in Chelyabinsk) was no longer required to produce T-34 tanks. As before, this meant that IS-2 and ISU production increased. The March quota went up from 250 vehicles to 275 (100 IS-2 tanks and 175 ISU-152 SPGs), 350 vehicles were due in April (150 IS-2, 130 ISU-152, 70 ISU-122), 400 in May (175 IS-2, 125 ISU-152, 100 ISU-122), 450 in June (200 IS-2, 130 ISU-152, 120 ISU-122), and starting with July 500 vehicles monthly (225 IS-2, 100 ISU-152, 175 ISU-122).[220]

Improved Armor

The tank's armor improved over the course of its production. Several new German armored vehicles with thicker armor and more powerful guns than seen before were discovered in the summer of 1943. The IS-2's armor was originally designed to withstand the Tiger's 88 mm KwK 36 L/56 gun, but it was no longer sufficient to resist the more powerful 88 mm Pak 43 L/71 used on the Ferdinand and 75 mm Kwk 42 L/70 used on the Panther.[221]

Work on transitioning from medium hardness to high hardness armor began back in 1943, and experience gained in previous designs was

---

[218] A.G. Solyankin and others, *Sovetskiye tyazheliye tanki 1941-1945*, Tseyghaus, Moscow, 2007, p.59
[219] A.G. Solyankin and others, *Sovetskiye tyazheliye tanki 1941-1945*, Tseyghaus, Moscow, 2007, p.60
[220] RGASPI F.644 Op.2 D.295 L.32
[221] M. Postnikov, *Bronezaschita Tyazhelikh Tankov KV i IS 1941-1945*, Eksprint, Moscow, 2006, p. 28-29

subsequently applied to the IS-2.[222] Instead of the old medium hardness armor, new turrets, front hull sections, and commander's cupolas were cast from high hardness 70L steel starting in March of 1944. This armor reduced the maximum distance at which the tank could be penetrated by the Panther's 75 mm KwK 42 gun to 900-1100 meters.[223] In comparison, the IS-2's D-25T gun could effectively combat the Panther at ranges of 2 kilometers,[224] giving a comfortable margin of safety when fighting the German tank. The high hardness armor also improved protection against 88 mm guns. Trials showed that the difference in the limit of penetration at an angle of 17-18 degrees (the angle of an IS-2's turret side) was about 100 m/s, which corresponded to a distance of 1500 m for an armor piercing shell with a ballistic cap.[225] The resilience of the high hardness turrets under heavy fire was also higher. The turret made of 70L high hardness steel took 11 hits to the side and 6 hits to the rear from 88 mm guns in trials without cracking.[226] Various other minor improvements such as new tow hooks and improved ammunition racks were gradually introduced in the spring of 1944. New handrails for infantry riders were added in July, and spare track links were moved from the rear of the hull to the lower front. The wider gun mantlet was also introduced sometime in July. These changes were also implemented on early production IS-2 tanks that went through refurbishment.[227]

---

[222] RGAE F.8752 Op.4 D.303 L.121
[223] TsAMO RF F.38 Op.11355 D.2243 L.158
[224] TsAMO RF F.307 Op.4148 D.189 L.107
[225] RGAE F.8752 Op.7 D.11 L.12
[226] RGAE F.8752 Op.7 D.11 L.13
[227] Y. Pasholok, *Borba za mesto na konveyere*, https://warspot.ru/11457-borba-za-mesto-na-konveyere, retrieved on May 27th, 2021

Spare track links were moved from the rear to the front of IS-2 tanks in July of 1944. Patriot Park. *(Pavel Borovikov)*

Another major change was coming to the IS-2. GKO decree #5583ss signed on April 8th, 1944, called for a more radical increase in protection than simply switching to a new alloy.[228] The requirements were open to interpretation, and ChKZ's SKB-2 (Kirov Factory in Chelyabinsk Specialized Design Bureau #2) decided to improve protection by changing the shape of the hull.[229] The existing shape of the IS-2 hull was not much different than what the KV-1 had five years prior. A characteristic "step" in the front armor housing the driver's vision port was less angled than the rest of the front armor, thus weakening the tank's frontal protection. A more reasonable approach was to develop a flat upper front hull, similar to what was used on the T-34. This would result in a hull that was better protected and easier to produce. The

[228] RGASPI F.644 Op.2 D.305 L.144

[229] M. Postnikov, *Bronezaschita Tyazhelikh Tankov KV i IS 1941-1945*, Eksprint, Moscow, 2006, p. 29

upper front armor was 90 mm thick if rolled or 100 mm thick if cast, positioned at an angle of 60 degrees from vertical. The lower front armor was 90 mm thick if rolled and 120-130 mm thick if cast, positioned at 30 degrees from vertical. The driver's vision port was removed and replaced with a new fixed observation device. The new hull design was finished on April 14th, 1944.[230] Photos of the different hull designs can be seen in the Chapter Anatomy of a Heavy Tank, Section Hull.

IS-2 tank with an original style hull, Patriot Park. The upper section of the hull is broken into two distinct sections with a very steeply sloped middle part and much more vertical upper part that houses the driver's vision port. *(Pavel Borovikov)*

[230] Y. Pasholok, *Malaya modernizatsiya bolshogo tanka*, https://warspot.ru/12831-malaya-modernizatsiya-bolshogo-tanka, retrieved on May 29th, 2021

IS-2 tank with a type of hull adopted in 1944, IWM Duxford. The upper front section of this hull is straightened and composed of only one section sloped at 60 degrees. (Peter Samsonov)

Preparations for mass production began in May of 1944. UZTM (Ural Heavy Machinebuilding Factory) produced its first hulls in May, factory #200 produced its first four hulls in June.[231] ChKZ (Kirov Factory in Chelyabinsk) began assembling IS-2 tanks with the new hull in July of 1944, although a backlog of old hulls still existed and was only fully used up in August. It is difficult to tell the exact date of this transition as the tanks with the new hulls were not distinguished from the old ones by name. In some cases, the new tanks were called "IS-2 with a straightened front" (IS so spryamlennym nosom).[232] To date, the author has not encountered a period document where modern terms "IS-2 model 1943" and "IS-2 model 1944" were used.

Malyshev ordered UZTM (Ural Heavy Machinebuilding Factory) and factory #200 to deliver hulls to the NIBT Proving Grounds for trials on May 10th, 1944, but this did not happen until September, long after this type of hull entered production.[233] Fortunately, trials showed that these hulls were superior to their predecessor. The upper front armor of the rolled steel hull produced at UZTM could not be penetrated by the Panther's 75 mm KwK 42 L/70 gun at any range.[234] The lower front armor was vulnerable from 1.5 km. The upper armor deflected the 88 mm Pak 43 at ranges of 450 m or more, but the lower front could be penetrated at effectively any distance.[235] The hull cast at factory #200 performed much better: the Pak 43 was capable of penetrating the upper armor only in some cases at 225 meters. The penetration distance of the lower front was also reduced, for instance the Panther's gun could only penetrate it from 785 meters. The welding seams showed damage after nonpenetrating hits, but factory #200's hull was better than

[231] Y. Pasholok, Malaya modernizatsiya bolshogo tanka, https://warspot.ru/12831-malaya-modernizatsiya-bolshogo-tanka, retrieved on May 29th, 2021
[232] TsAMO RF F.38 Op.11355 D.2245 L.240-241
[233] Y. Pasholok, Malaya modernizatsiya bolshogo tanka, https://warspot.ru/12831-malaya-modernizatsiya-bolshogo-tanka, retrieved on May 29th, 2021
[234] TsAMO RF F.38 Op.11355 D.2243 L.158
[235] TsAMO RF F.38 Op.11355. D.2872 L.15

UZTM's in this regard as well.[236] Quality control trials performed in 1945 showed that this defect was eventually eliminated.[237] The tradeoff for this improved protection was decrease in visibility. The new driver's observation device offered a greater vision range than the old observation one, but it was no longer possible to open the observation port outside of combat for a better field of view. Work was performed to mitigate this drawback, and even though a wider opening for the driver's observation device was approved, it was never implemented.[238] Only one change was made to improve the driver's vision: the MK-IV observation periscopes were slightly shifted forward. The tanks continued to change even after the new hull was introduced. A barrel clamp was added to the rear of the hull starting on September 1st, 1944. A new inertial starter was installed starting on September 20th.[239]

Incremental changes were made not just to the tank's design, but also the production schedule. New quotas were set on August 9th, 1944. According to GKO decree #6345ss, ChKZ (Kirov Factory in Chelyabinsk, *Chelyabinskiy Kirovskiy Zavod*) was now expected to produce 250 IS-2 tanks, 100 ISU-152 SPGs, and 150 ISU-122 SPGs monthly. The total number of chassis remained the same, but instead of 25 ISU-122s, the factory was building 25 IS-2 tanks.[240] Production quotas were revised again on January 18th, 1945. GKO decree #7332ss again kept the total number of chassis the same, but the amount of ISU-122 produced was briefly reduced, this time in favor of the ISU-152. 110 ISU-152s and 140 ISU-122s were expected monthly in January, but then returning to 100 and 150 respectively by February.[241]

---

[236] Y. Pasholok, *Malaya modernizatsiya bolshogo tanka*, https://warspot.ru/12831-malaya-modernizatsiya-bolshogo-tanka, retrieved on May 29th, 2021

[237] TsAMO RF F.38 Op.11369 D.581 L.12

[238] Y. Pasholok, *Dolgoigrayushiy IS*, https://warspot.ru/17113-dolgoigrayuschiy-is, retrieved on September 26th, 2022

[239] Y. Pasholok, *Malaya modernizatsiya bolshogo tanka*, https://warspot.ru/12831-malaya-modernizatsiya-bolshogo-tanka, retrieved on May 29th, 2021

[240] RGASPI F.644 Op.1. D.292 L.47

[241] RGASPI F.644 Op.1 D.350 L.27

The next major change was implemented in November. This change was authorized by GKO (State Committee of Defense) decree #6723ss signed by Stalin on October 14th, 1944. The decree called for installation of an AA mount for the 12.7 mm DShK *(Dyegtyaryev-Shpagin Krupnokaliberniy*, Dyegryaryev-Shpagin high caliber) machine gun on the turret of IS tanks and casemates of ISU SPGs. The first 25 such mounts were installed on 25 ISU-122S SPGs in October of 1944 and the first 25 IS-2 tanks received them in November. 125 IS-2 tanks received this mount in December and starting with January of 1945 all IS-2 tanks were produced with DShK machine guns.[242]

A DShK 12.7 mm machine gun on an anti-aircraft mount was installed on IS-2 tanks starting in October of 1944. *(Pavel Borovikov)*

Production was revised once more in March of 1945. Improvements made to protection introduced in the spring-summer of 1944 were only

[242] RGASPI F.644 Op.1 D.323 L.42

half-measures, as the upper front hull armor of the IS-2 tank did not offer complete protection against the German 88 mm Pak 43 L/71.[243] A radical redesign was needed in order to make the tank fully proof against this and more powerful prospective weapons. This vehicle was indexed Object 703 and accepted into service as the IS-3 (reusing the designation IS-3 first given to the Object 237 in 1943).[244] GKO (State Committee of Defense) decree #7950ss signed by Stalin on March 29th called for the delivery of the first 25 production IS-3s and 225 IS-2 tanks in April of 1945. The proportion continued to shift towards the IS-3: IS-3s would be delivered in May 100 compared to just 150 IS-2s, in June the IS-2 would be phased out of production entirely at ChKZ (Kirov Factory in Chelyabinsk) and 250 IS-3s were expected. The quotas for the ISU-152 and ISU-122 SPGs did not change: 100 and 150 respectively were expected monthly.[245] 3385 IS-2 tanks were produced at ChKZ in total before production ended.[246]

ChKZ (Kirov Factory in Chelyabinsk) was not the only manufacturer of IS-2 tanks. The Soviet government was eager to set up a second manufacturing base for the Red Army's new heavy tank. GKO (State Committee of Defense) decree #5959ss signed by Stalin on May 26th, 1944, called for the restoration of the LKZ (Kirov Factory in Leningrad).[247] The Izhora factory would also be rebuilt to supply the LKZ with hulls and turrets. The first 10 tanks were expected in October of 1944, 20 in November, 25 in December, and then 50 monthly starting in January of 1945. The factory was also tasked with refurbishing up to 35 KV tanks per month and production of 1.5 million rubles worth of spare parts per month by the end of 1944.[248]

---

[243] TsAMO RF F.38 Op.11355 D.2872 L.15

[244] TsAMO RF F.38 Op.11355 D.1377 L. 173

[245] RGASPI F.644 Op.2 D.464 L.82-83

[246] Y. Pasholok, *IS-2 Argument Kalibrom 122 mm*, https://warspot.ru/4016-is-2-argument-kalibrom-122-mm, retrieved on August 26th, 2022

[247] Y. Pasholok, Malaya modernizatsiya bolshogo tanka, https://warspot.ru/12831-malaya-modernizatsiya-bolshogo-tanka, retrieved on May 29th, 2021

[248] RGASPI F.644 Op.2. D.338 L.52

This was easier said than done. LKZ (Kirov Factory in Leningrad) remained functional during the blockade of the city maintained by German and Finnish forces from September 1941 to January 1944, although it suffered significant damage. Many of its workers were either evacuated or killed, and a lot of equipment went missing. It was still in better condition than the Izhora factory, which saw battles inside its walls more than once. As October drew closer it became more and more clear that these quotas would be impossible to meet, and on October 14th, 1944, GKO decree #6706ss delayed the start of production until December, when 5 tanks would be expected.[249] Even these plans proved too optimistic. The first five tanks were assembled in March of 1945 using components originally built in early 1944. These tanks were only delivered in June. Five other tanks were delivered in May. Production of IS-2 tanks at LKZ ceased with just 10 vehicles delivered.[250]

[249] RGASPI F.644 Op.1 D.317 L.1-2

[250] Y. Pasholok, *Malaya modernizatsiya bolshogo tanka*, https://warspot.ru/12831-malaya-modernizatsiya-bolshogo-tanka, retrieved on May 29th, 2021

Table 1: IS Tank Production Quotas[251] (Chelyabinsk Kirov Factory)[252]

	IS-1	IS-2	ISU-152	ISU-122	IS-3
November 1943	25	10	5	-	-
December 1943	75 40*	35	30	-	-
January 1944	40	35	50	-	-
February 1944	-	75	75	-	-
March 1944	-	100	150 175**	-	-
April 1944	-	150	150 130**	- 70**	-
May 1944	-	175	125	100	-
June 1944	-	200	130	120	-
July 1944	-	225	100	175	-
August 1944	-	250	75 100***	200 150***	-
September 1944	-	250	100	150	-
October 1944	-	250	100	150	-
November 1944	-	250	100	150	-
December 1944	-	250	100	150	-
January 1945	-	250	110	140	-
February 1945	-	250	100	150	-
March 1945	-	250	100	150	-
April 1945	-	225	100	150	25
Total wartime****	105	3230	1730	1805	25
May 1945	-	150	100	150	100
June 1945	-	-	100	150	250

* Quota reduced by GKO decree #4043ss, which accepted the IS-2 into service.
** Quota changed by GKO decree #5378ss, which removed the T-34 from production at ChKZ.
*** Quota changed by GKO decree #6345ss.
**** The Great Patriotic War ended on May 9th, 1945. For the purposes of this table, tanks produced in May do not count as wartime production quotas.

---

[251] Actual delivery lagged behind quota. Tanks in one month's quota were often officially accepted by the customer early in the next month.
[252] Almost all IS-2 tanks were built at the Chelyabinsk Kirov Factory, with the exception of 10 tanks built at the Leningrad Kirov Factory in 1945.

Still not Big Enough?

The IS-2 was the most heavily armed and armored tank in the Red Army at the time of its adoption, but it was still considered unsatisfactory to the army in many ways. Investigations into ways to improve the tank began as soon as it was accepted into service.

Improving the Armor

The armor of the tank was designed to protect against the 88 mm KwK 36 L/56 gun, but information about the more powerful 75 mm KwK 42 L/70 and 88 mm Pak 43 L/71 guns came to light between the start of the design and acceptance of this tank. In April of 1944, NIBT Proving Grounds staff made a proposal to straighten the upper front hull, but keep the thickness at 120 mm. The lower front armor would be reduced in thickness to 75 mm to save on weight. The sides of the hull would be thinned out to 75 mm from 90 mm, but they would be built from rolled armor rather than cast. Resistance would also be improved by sloping them at 45 degrees rather than the original 15 degrees.[253] Out of all of these suggestions only the shape of the front hull was put into production.[254]

The improved hull shape introduced a new problem. Chief Engineer at factory #200 Nitsenko wrote a letter to Kotin and Chief of the GBTU (Main Armored Vehicle Directorate) Tank Directorate Major General Afonin on June 21st, 1944, arguing that it should be removed entirely. His reasoning was that the old IS-2 hull had a relatively small opening for the machine gun. The new hull shape caused the opening to stretch out and negatively impact the toughness of the armor in that section. Nitsenko argued that since it was impossible to aim the bow machine

---

[253] TsAMO RF F.38 Op.11355 D.2369 L.24-26
[254] A.G. Solyankin and others, Sovietskiye Tyazheliye Tanki 1917-1941, Tseyghaus, Moscow, 2006, p.62

gun it served no purpose in the tank and weakened its armor for no benefit.[255]

Factory #100 pitched a much more radical modernization of the armor designed by Shashmurin. The designer estimated that at a weight of 55-56 tons he could provide it with enough armor to completely protect it from German 75 and 88 mm guns from the front and all but close distances from the sides. This was less a modernization of an existing tank and more of a new model, designed to compete with ChKZ's (Kirov Factory in Chelyabinsk) Object 701 (future IS-4).[256]

Factory #100 also proposed a more conservative improvement. The upper and lower hull front armor was thickened to 120 mm, with the sides 75 mm thick. The turret front and sides were 150 mm thick with the rear at 100 mm. This tank was estimated to weigh 46-47 tons. Despite this increase in weight the top speed was estimated at 50 kph. No engine is specified in the proposal, but it would have to be a more powerful one than the 520 hp V-2-IS. Wooden models of this tank were built, showing variants with either a fully cast hull in the shape of an elongated upturned bowl or a welded hull with two separate upper front plates, installed at an angle to one another. This position of plates is often called "pike nose".[257]

Strangely enough, factory #100 first started working on the latter variant, but then abandoned it in favor of the former one. Meanwhile, their competitors at ChKZ worked on a modernized IS-2 as ordered. Their tank was given the blueprint index 703 and name Kirovets-1, which was later changed to IS-3.[258] This tank was an offshoot of the Object 701 program and implemented many improvements developed

[255] TsAMO RF F.38 Op.11355 D.2245 L.240-241ß
[256] Y. Pasholok, *Ne popavshiy v amplitudu*, https://warspot.ru/15654-ne-popavshiy-v-amplitudu, retrieved on June 6th, 2021
[257] Y. Pasholok, *Modernizatsia na bumage*, https://warspot.ru/12111-modernizatsiya-na-bumage, retrieved on June 6th, 2021
[258] RGASPI F.644 Op.2 D.464 L.86

for that tank. Factory #100 reacted to their rivals by designing the IS-2U, a tank very similar to the original IS-2 but with the pike nose front hull shape developed by V.I. Tarotko. The IS-2U was never built in metal, but this hull shape was used in building the production IS-3 tank.[259] Even though the tank was described as "a modernized IS-2" in GKO (State Committee of Defense) decree #7950, it was in many ways a brand new tank.[260]

Improving the Gun

The IS-2's gun was also found wanting. The separate loading[261] process increased the number of steps required to load the gun. It would be natural to expect the reduction of the number of steps to increase the rate of fire, and so fixed ammunition that could be loaded in one motion was developed. The first attempt to build a D-25 gun that used fixed ammunition was undertaken on the T-44 tank. A prototype with an 1800 mm wide turret ring was built and tested in February of 1944.[262] The D-25-44 gun installed on the tank was similar to the IS-2's D-25T, but its muzzle velocity was 2-3% lower due to reduction of the casing volume and amount of propellant. Trials showed that the rate of fire was only 2-3 RPM.[263] While this spelled the end of the D-25-44, attempts to develop fixed ammunition for the D-25T gun continued. GKO decree #6868s issued on November 4th, 1944, called for increasing the rate of fire of the D-25T gun, including the development of fixed

[259] Y. Pasholok, *Morda klinom dlya tyazhelogo tanka*, https://zen.yandex.ru/media/yuripasholok/morda-klinom-dlia-tiajelogo-tanka-5f7eb0a715099c198a02f2f6, retrieved on June 6th, 2021
[260] RGASPI F.644 Op.2 D.464 L.86
[261] In separate loading, the shell is loaded into the breech first, followed by the propellant casing.
[262] Y. Pasholok, *Shag v nuzhnom napravlenii*, https://warspot.ru/14932-shag-v-nuzhnom-napravlenii, retrieved on September 28th, 2022
[263] Y. Pasholok, *Slishkom dlinniy unitar*, https://zen.yandex.ru/media/yuripasholok/slishkom-dlinnyi-unitar-5fba3e769d2ffe38ee7d8cda, retrieved on June 6th, 2021.

ammunition.[264] As a result of these orders, NII-24 developed fixed rounds for the fully fledged D-25T gun used in the IS-2 tank. The new ammunition was not very promising, as the length of the AP round was 1203 mm and the HE round was even longer, 1393 mm. The complete round weighed 40 kg.[265] Trials were carried out on January 14-15th in an IS-2 tank and an ISU-122 SPG. The results were anything but an increase in the rate of fire. The long and heavy fixed round was even more difficult to load than ammunition already in mass production.[266] The situation in the IS-2 was worse than in the SPG, as it was impossible to load the gun at elevations greater than 10 degrees as the casing fouled the turret ring. The gun in the production tank could be loaded at any angle. The only benefit from this change was that the ISU-122 could now carry 34 rounds of ammunition instead of 30, but the IS-2's ammunition capacity dropped from 28 to 27 rounds. The GBTU issued their verdict on January 26th, 1945: fixed ammunition[267] solves no problems and only causes new ones. The new fixed round was almost 1400 mm long and weighed 40 kg, which made it very difficult to handle in the limited space available inside a tank.[268] The GAU (*Glavnoye Artilleriyskoye Upravleniye*, Main Artillery Directorate) made its own verdict in April of 1945. In their opinion, there could be no benefit in this style of ammunition over the existing separate loading system unless the length of the complete round could be reduced to 1000 mm or less. This was not the end of the quest for fixed ammunition, and work stopped only on Malyshev's categorical refusal to even attempt development of such a project for the IS-3.[269]

---

[264] RGASPI F.644 Op.1 D.330 L.115

[265] Y. Pasholok, *Slishkom dlinniy unitar*, https://zen.yandex.ru/media/yuripasholok/slishkom-dlinnyi-unitar-5fba3e769d2ffe38ee7d8cda, retrieved on June 6th, 2021.

[266] TsAMO RF F.38 Op.11369 D.696 L.46

[267] Fixed ammunition is loaded as one unit with the shell inserted into the propellant casing at the factory.

[268] TsAMO RF F.38 Op.11369 D.696 L.47

[269] Y. Pasholok, *Slishkom dlinniy unitar*, https://zen.yandex.ru/media/yuripasholok/slishkom-dlinnyi-unitar-5fba3e769d2ffe38ee7d8cda, retrieved on June 6th, 2021.

Maybe a Smaller Size?

The goal of improving the rate of fire also went in a different direction. If the size of the ammunition was a problem, then the solution lay in a smaller caliber gun with a higher muzzle velocity. Good candidates for this replacement already existed. For instance, the 100 mm 412-1V tank gun based on the ballistics of the B-34[270] naval gun was pitched by LKZ (Kirov Factory in Leningrad) in January of 1941.[271] The idea was turned down at the time, as land artillery did not use this caliber and there was no armor piercing ammunition available.[272] The concept of a 100 mm tank gun languished until May 5th, 1943, when Stalin signed GKO (State Committee of Defense) decree #3290ss. The decree called for the development of several new weapons, including "A 100 mm corps gun with the ballistics of the B-34 naval AA gun (muzzle velocity of 900 m/s, 15.6 kg shell, maximum range 22 km)."[273] Development of a 100 mm AP shell was also ordered.[274]

The idea of installing a 100 mm gun into a tank wasn't far behind. As with 122 mm tank guns, the TsAKB (Central Artillery Design Bureau) and factory #9 stepped up with a project. A lighter shell with a higher muzzle velocity would have given slightly lower penetration than the D-25T, but the increased rate of fire could make the tradeoff worth it.[275] The topic of installing a 100 mm gun into the turret of an IS tank appears in the list of experimental work for the NKV (People's Commissariat of Armament) and the GAU (Main Artillery Directorate) for 1944.[276]

---

[270] The letter B in the designation indicates that the gun was developed at the Bolshevik factory in Leningrad.
[271] TsAMO RF F.81 Op.12104 D.201 L.11-12
[272] Y. Pasholok, *Optimalnaya modernizatsiya*, https://warspot.ru/13911-optimalnaya-modernizatsiya, retrieved on June 6th, 2021
[273] RGASPI F.644 Op.2 D.156 L.92
[274] RGASPI F.644 Op.2 D.156 L.93
[275] TsAMO RF F.38 Op.11369 D.490 L.35
[276] RGASPI F.644 Op.2 D.254 L.177-181

There were once again two competing designs, one from factory #9 and the other from the TsAKB (Central Artillery Design Bureau). Factory #9's 100 mm D-10T gun was easy to install in an IS-1 turret and did not require radical alteration of the gun mount or fighting compartment.[277] The tank with this gun was indexed Object 245 or IS-4 (not to be confused with the Object 701, which was accepted into service as the IS-4 in 1946).[278]

Preliminary trials were held in April of 1944. The tank reached a practical rate of fire of 7.5 RPM in trials.[279] A report composed on April 12th listed a number of issues with the new fighting compartment, largely to do with ventilation, location of the optics, and ammunition storage.[280]

On April 27th, before these defects were corrected, Malyshev wrote a letter to Beria asking him to pen a draft GKO decree to accept this gun into production. The practical rate of fire of the gun was 2-3 times higher than that of the IS-2 with a D-25T gun. The lack of muzzle brake reduced obscuration after firing and made the tank less noticeable, while also making life easier for infantry that might have to follow the tank closely. The D-10T was 300-400 kg lighter than the D-25T and more compact, which made the fighting compartment roomier. The penetration of the D-10T was slightly higher than that of the D-25T at ranges under 1000 m.[281]

Follow-up trials were held on July 1-3rd, 1944. The trials commission concluded that the drawbacks of the D-10T gun and the fighting compartment of the IS tank were largely mitigated. The gun could be recommended for service with the Red Army.[282]

---

[277] TsAMO RF F.38 Op.11369 D.490 L.35
[278] M. Baryatinskiy, *Tyazheliy tank IS-2*, Yauza, Moscow, 2006, pp.29-30
[279] TsAMO RF F.38 Op.11355 D.2375 L.17
[280] TsAMO RF F.38 Op.11369 D.28 L.17-17 (reverse)
[281] TsAMO RF F.38 Op.11369 D.490 L.36
[282] TsAMO RF F.38 Op.11369 D.28 L.3

Factory #9 appeared to have scored an easy victory, but that was not the case. The Commander of Artillery of the Red Army Marshal Voronov and Head of the GAU (Main Artillery Directorate) Marshal Yakovlev spoke out against this decision. In their opinion, the penetration of the gun was insufficient at ranges over 1000 m, and mass production had to be delayed until this gap was closed. They also pointed out that the high explosive ammunition of the 122 mm D-25T was very effective, whereas the 100 mm D-10T would have a smaller shell with worse explosive and fragmentation effects. The semiautomatic mechanism also required more work. Voronov and Yakovlev were all for replacing the D-5S gun on the SU-85 with the new D-10, but preferred to keep the D-25T gun in the IS-2 tank due to its superior armor penetration and fragmentation effects.[283] Eventually the 100 mm D-10S gun was accepted into service as the armament of the SU-100, but the tank version was only used on medium tanks, not heavy ones.[284]

The gun designed by the TsAKB (Central Artillery Design Bureau) was indexed S-34[285] and could accept three different kinds of barrels: a 100 mm barrel with the ballistics of the B-34 gun, a 122 mm barrel with the ballistics of the A-19, and a third 85 mm variant with the muzzle velocity boosted to 1000-1100 m/s.[286] On December 27th, 1943, an order was given to install 100 mm guns into an IS tank and an SPG on the T-34 chassis by February 20th, 1944, complete acceptance trials, and deliver the final verdict regarding the production of this gun by March 5th, 1944.[287]

The new gun was finished on time and installed not in an IS tank, but a KV-85 tank.[288] Trials were held from January 22nd to the 28th, 1944.

---

[283] TsAMO RF F.38 Op.11369 D.490 L.37-38
[284] Y. Pasholok, *Optimalnaya modernizatsiya*, https://warspot.ru/13911-optimalnaya-modernizatsiya, retrieved on June 6th, 2021
[285] The letter S in the designation indicates that the gun was developed at the Central Artillery Design Bureau (TsAKB, *Tsentralnoye artilleriyskoye konstruktorskoye byuro*)
[286] RGASPI F.622 Op.2 D.254 L.178
[287] RGASPI F.622 Op.2 D.254 L.177
[288] TsAMO RF F.38 Op.11369 D.490 L.4-5

The trials indeed showed that the rate of fire increased compared to the D-25T. The peak rate of fire demonstrated was 12 RPM, although with a caveat: this was attained with the ammunition stacked in the turret bustle, as the ammunition racks were not converted. The sustained rate of fire with two groups of 10 shots each with closed hatches was 5.7-6.3 RPM, still an improvement over the D-25T. This boost came at a cost. The gun was less precise than its towed equivalent, the BS-3.[289] Aiming the gun was physically demanding. The fighting compartment was rearranged to accommodate the fact that the breech of the new gun opened to the right rather than to the left, but these changes were not sufficient. Even though the commander's cupola was moved to his new position to the right of the gun, he didn't have the benefit of the space provided to him by the cupola bulge, and so his position was quite cramped. The loader's position was also less comfortable than before.[290]

Despite its drawbacks, the S-34 gun performed well enough to be installed in a real IS tank. This tank was indexed Object 248 or IS-5 (not to be confused with the Object 730, also indexed IS-5 and later renamed first to IS-8 and then T-10). A prototype was completed in June of 1944 and tested between July 1st and 6th. Unlike the D-10, the S-34 failed trials. The breech, semiautomatic mechanism, and recoil mechanisms needed more work. Furthermore, the layout of the turret needed to be redesigned in order to accept the new gun.[291] Precision of the S-34 was also considerably poorer than that of the D-10T.[292]

The vehicle was still sent back for improvements. By October the turret was altered to give the commander more space, ammunition capacity

---

[289] The letters BS in the designation indicate the contribution of the Bolshevik factory (B) and Central Artillery Design Bureau (TsAKB, *Tsentralnoye artilleriyskoye konstruktorskoye byuro*) to the design.
[290] Y. Pasholok, *KV ne hochet uhodit*, https://warspot.ru/11571-kv-ne-hochet-uhodit, retrieved on June 6th, 2021
[291] TsAMO RF F.38 Op.11369 D.28 L.3
[292] TsAMO RF F.38 Op.11369 D.28 L.36 (reverse)

was increased to 39 rounds, and a stabilized sight and mechanical gun rammer were added. The tank passed trials held in the fall.[293]

The TsAKB (Central Artillery Design Bureau) appeared to have recovered from their failure, but their effort was futile. It turned out that the 100 mm caliber did not come without disadvantages. For instance, while the limit of complete penetration of the Panther's upper front plate was about 1300-1400 m for the D-10, the D-25 could penetrate it at a range of over 2 kilometers.[294] In addition to penetration of the armor, a hit from a 122 mm shell resulted in significant spalling and cracking of the armor, while penetrations of the 100 mm shell rarely caused cracks and only produced minimal spalling.[295] The gain in rate of fire was also not as significant as previously thought, as the D-25S with a semiautomatic breech installed in the ISU-122S SPG reached a rate of fire of 6 RPM, and the IS-2's rate of fire similarly increased.[296] Overall, Yakovlev spoke out against the decision to replace the 122 mm gun with a 100 mm one, at least until a 100 mm armor piercing shell could be developed that allowed the latter to achieve superior performance to the former. In the same letter, Yakovlev writes that even in its current state the performance of the 100 mm D-10 was superior to that of the 85 mm D-5, and so work on installation of 100 mm guns into medium tanks and SPGs would continue.[297] Further development of Soviet armored vehicles continued along this path, with heavy tanks up to the T-10 retaining derivatives of the 122 mm D-25T[298] and medium tanks up to the T-55 using derivatives of the D-10T.[299]

[293] M. Baryatinskiy, *Tyazheliy tank IS-2*, Yauza, Moscow, 2006, pp.29-30
[294] TsAMO RF F.38 Op.11355 D.2375 L.3
[295] TsAMO RF F.38 Op.11355 D.2375 L.10-16
[296] TsAMO RF F.38 Op.11369 D.1 L.72
[297] TsAMO RF F.38 Op.11369 D.490 L.37-38
[298] Y. Pasholok, *Posledniy sovetskiy tyazhoeloves*, https://warspot.ru/4474-posledniy-sovetskiy-tyazheloves, retrieved on July 28th, 2022
[299] S. Shumilin and others, *Sredniy Tank T-55 (object 155)*, ZAO Redatsiya Zhurnala Modelist-Konstruktor, Moscow, 2008 p.20

More Ammo

Since the tank's low ammunition capacity (only 28 rounds) was a noticeable drawback, the NIBT Proving Grounds devised a means of storing three additional rounds of 122 mm gun ammunition. 3 shells and one propellant casing were stored on the floor of the fighting compartment on top of the regular bins held down with straps. Another casing fit in the front of the fighting compartment in the corner, a third in the pannier on the right. This solution was criticized as the ammunition was not protected from dirt or damage when stored in this way. A recommendation was given to equip 150 IS-2 tanks with extra ammunition stowage for testing purposes.[300] This solution was not recommended for use in mass production, although units in the field found their own ways to carry additional ammunition.[301]

Improving the Machine Gun

The tank's main armament was not the only weapon that was a candidate for an upgrade. People's Commissar of Armaments Dmitry Fedorovich Ustinov ordered the improvement of the IS-2's coaxial machine gun on February 17th, 1945. Two proposals were completed in July of 1945: one with a 12.7 mm DShK and one with a 14.5 mm KPV-44 (*Krupnokaliberniy pulemyet Vladimirova*, Vladimirov high caliber machine gun).[302] The coaxial DShK would be fed from 50 round belts that were either contained in drums or loaded freely. The machine gun and mount weighed 56 kg, the drum with a belt weighed 12 kg. A 105x75 mm opening would have to be cut into the gun mantlet to fit

---

[300] TsAMO RF F.38 Op.11355 D.2218 L.72-32 reproduced in A.M. Radionov and others, *Glavnoye Avtobronetankovoye Upravleniye Lyudi, Sobytiya, Fakty v Dokumentakh 1944-1945 kniga IV*, Moscow, 2007, pp.62-63
[301] TsAMO RF F.3409 Op.1 D.6 L.200-201
[302] TsAMO RF F.81 Op.12038 D.577 L.28

this machine gun.[303] The KPV-44 machine gun was fed by a freely hanging belt. The mount alone weighed 42 kg without the gun.[304]

Improving the Engine

Another aspect in which the IS-2 tank was not up to the army's expectations was the engine. As mentioned above, requirements for the KV-13 originally called for a 600 hp engine.[305] This requirement did not change for its successors, and yet the IS-1 was accepted into mass production with the 520 hp V-2-IS engine. This was considered acceptable as the tank demonstrated sufficient speed even at the lower output, but only as a temporary measure. Decree #4043 that accepted the IS-1 into production also called for the development of three new powerful engines: the V-6 that would output 800 hp at 2100 RPM and 600 hp at 1900-2000 RPM, the V-12, a supercharged V-2 that would output 800 hp at 2200 RPM and 650 hp at 1900-2000 RPM, and the M-30 that would produce 1100-1200 hp thanks to its centrifugal supercharger.[306]

This work reached success not too long after. GKO (State Committee of Defense) decree #5378 signed on March 12th, 1944, accepted the V-11 tank engine into service.[307] This engine achieved an output of 700 hp at 2200 RPM or 620 hp at 2100 RPM.[308] The dimensions of this engine were identical to that of the V-2-IS and it could be installed into the IS-1 and IS-2 tanks.[309] Production was due to start in June of 1944 with 75 units per month, then 250 in July and 400 in August.[310]

---

[303] TsAMO RF F.81 Op.12038 D.577 L.29-29 (reverse)
[304] TsAMO RF F.81 Op.12038 D.577 L.30-31
[305] RGASPI F.644 Op.2 D.69 L.74
[306] RGASPI F.644 Op.2 D.211 L.6
[307] RGASPI F.644 Op.2 D.295 L.34
[308] RGASPI F.644 Op.2 D.295 L.39
[309] RGASPI F.644 Op.1 D.313 L.131
[310] RGASPI F.644 Op.2 D.295 L.34

Increasing a tank's engine power without changing any of the other components proved to be a difficult task, and so Beria, Malyshev, and Fedorenko petitioned Stalin for a compromise. According to them, the NKTP (People's Commissariat of Tank Production) was working on adapting IS tanks and ISU SPGs to use a 580 hp variant of the engine. In the meantime, as the V-11 proved more reliable than the V-2, it could replace the V-2-IS in existing tanks without much of an issue. Stalin approved the proposal on October 10th, 1944, but the V-11 engine was never installed in IS-2 tanks, although it was used on the IS-3.[311]

---

[311] RGASPI F.644 Op.2 D.395 L.1-2

Anatomy of a Heavy Tank

This chapter is based on *Tyazheliy Tank. Rukovodstvo*, the manual for the IS-2 tank written by A.G. Kokin and other lecturers at the Chelyabinsk Tank Technical School published in early 1944 by the Military Publisher of the People's Commissariat of Defense in Moscow . Where necessary, the contents of the manual are annotated with information from secondary sources. Unless otherwise stated, this chapter describes an early IS-2 tank (curved upper front hull, D-25T gun with a screw breech and "Ferdinand style" muzzle brake, 10T-17 and PT4-17 sights).

The IS-2 heavy tank is a fully tracked armored vehicle with a rotating turret designed for assaulting heavily fortified positions as well as combat against enemy personnel, artillery, and armored vehicles.[312]

The Hull

The floor of the hull is assembled from two plates that are welded together. The seam between them runs across the center of the fighting compartment. There are 12 cutouts for torsion bar carriers made in the floor as well as 9 cutouts for drainage of oil, water, and fuel and 3 cutouts for hatches. One of the hatches is located behind the driver and can be used by the crew to exit the tank. One hatch is located underneath the engine and is used for maintenance of the fuel and oil pumps. The third hatch is located under the main clutch and is also used for adjustment and maintenance.[313]

---

[312] A.G. Kokin and others, *Tyazheliy Tank. Rukovodstvo*, Military Publisher of the People's Commissariat of Defense, Moscow, 1944, p.3
[313] A.G. Kokin and others, *Tyazheliy Tank. Rukovodstvo*, Military Publisher of the People's Commissariat of Defense, Moscow, 1944, p.26-28

Belly plate of an IS-2 tank on display in Nizhnekamsk. Many of the original hatch lids are missing. *(Nikita Trutnev)*

The front of the hull is cast in one piece and welded to the floor, hull superstructure, and lower vertical hull plates. Two tow hooks with sprung clips are welded to the lower part of the hull front. Carriers for the idlers are welded to the left and right of the front hull casting.[314] As of June 15th, 1944, six spare track links are carried on the lower part of the front hull.[315] A driver's observation port is installed in the center of the top section of the hull front casting. The observation port can be closed with a plug. The plug contains an observation slit, protected by a block of triplex tempered glass. The plug can be locked in the open or closed position. A torsion bar is installed to make opening and closing it easier. Openings for two periscopes are included to the left and right of the observation port. These are used to improve the driver's visibility if the observation port is closed. The periscopes can rotate and tilt and can

[314] A.G. Kokin and others, *Tyazheliy Tank. Rukovodstvo*, Military Publisher of the People's Commissariat of Defense, Moscow, 1944, p.29-30
[315] A.G. Solyankin and others, *Sovetskiye tyazheliye tanki 1941-1945*, Tseyghaus, Moscow, 2007, p.60

be locked in place.[316] A headlight is located on the front of the hull, to the right side.[317] A horn is located to the right of the headlight.[318]

Starting in July 1944 IS-2 tanks were assembled with the new "straightened front" type hull. This hull did not have an observation port in the front, only a fixed observation slit protected with triplex tempered glass and an armored cap.[319]

IS-2 tank with an early type hull, Patriot Park. The driver's observation device on this type of tank could swing out and give the driver a larger field of vision on the march. *(Pavel Borovikov)*

---

[316] A.G. Kokin and others, *Tyazheliy Tank. Rukovodstvo*, Military Publisher of the People's Commissariat of Defense, Moscow, 1944, p.29-32
[317] Note that the headlight position changed from right to left some time after the hull shape was changed. Be aware that in a post-war modernization IS-2s received two headlights.
[318] A.G. Kokin and others, *Tyazheliy Tank. Rukovodstvo*, Military Publisher of the People's Commissariat of Defense, Moscow, 1944, p.279
[319] Y. Pasholok, *Malaya modernizatsiya bolshogo tanka*, https://warspot.ru/12831-malaya-modernizatsiya-bolshogo-tanka, retrieved on May 29th, 2021

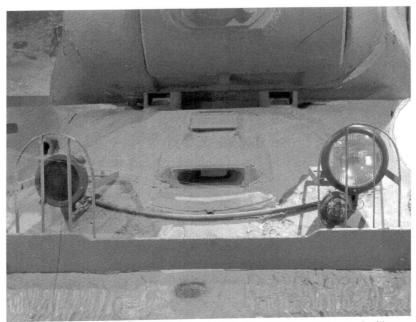

IS-2 tank with a late type hull, Museum of National Military History, Padikovo. The driver's observation device on this tank was immobile. *(Pavel Borovikov)*

The driver's compartment is located in the front of the hull. It contains the driver's seat as well as his controls and instruments. The instrument panel, two tanks of compressed air, flashlight rack, tachometer, horn, electric trigger for the rigidly mounted machine gun, an intercom system plug, and slots for some instruments are all located on the inside of the front hull casting.[320] The instrument panel is illuminated by two lights with a socket for a portable backup lamp on the right side of the compartment.[321] An evacuation hatch is installed in the floor of the tank, behind the driver's seat.[322] There are two fuel tanks in the driver's

[320] A.G. Kokin and others, *Tyazheliy Tank. Rukovodstvo*, Military Publisher of the People's Commissariat of Defense, Moscow, 1944, p.29
[321] A.G. Kokin and others, *Tyazheliy Tank. Rukovodstvo*, Military Publisher of the People's Commissariat of Defense, Moscow, 1944, p.278
[322] A.G. Kokin and others, *Tyazheliy Tank. Rukovodstvo*, Military Publisher of the People's Commissariat of Defense, Moscow, 1944, p.4

compartment, the left one holds 245 L of fuel and the right one holds 190 L.[323]

Machine gun blister of the IS-2 tank on display in Nizhnekamsk. This machine gun was rigidly fixed and fired by the driver. A fake barrel is installed. *(Nikita Trutnev)*

The center of the hull consists of a cast turret platform that houses the turret ring. The sides of the hull consist of three parts: the sloped superstructure sides, the horizontal pannier floor, and the vertical lower hull plates. These plates are welded together. The left pannier houses ammunition for the main gun and machine guns, the right pannier houses electrical equipment.[324] A device for communicating with

[323] A.G. Kokin and others, *Tyazheliy Tank. Rukovodstvo*, Military Publisher of the People's Commissariat of Defense, Moscow, 1944. p.19
[324] A.G. Kokin and others, *Tyazheliy Tank. Rukovodstvo*, Military Publisher of the People's Commissariat of Defense, Moscow, 1944, pp.32-34

infantry that can be activated from outside the tank is located here.[325] The button to activate this device is located on the outside of the tank on the left side of the superstructure, between the external fuel tanks.[326] Running lights are located on the left and right side of the turret platform.[327] Six torsion bar carriers, six bump stops, three idler carriers, a mud scraper carrier, and a trunnion for the track tensioning mechanism are welded to the outside of the vertical sides of the hull.[328]

The Turret

The turret consists of a large casting that makes up the sides and rear, as well as a rolled roof that is welded on top. The roof consists of two pieces welded together. The front section of the roof has a small slope. This section contains an opening for the PT4-15 periscopic gun sight, a ventilation fan with a dome shaped cover, and the loader's observation periscope. The rear part of the roof contains the antenna port with a protective ring, the loader's hatch, and the commander's cupola. Pistol ports are included in the left and right side of the turret. The pistol ports are shut with armored plugs when not in use. An opening for the gun mount is left in the front of the turret. A machine gun ball mount is installed in the rear of the turret.[329] The rear machine gun is equipped with a PU optical sight.[330]

---

[325] A.G. Kokin and others, *Tyazheliy Tank. Rukovodstvo*, Military Publisher of the People's Commissariat of Defense, Moscow, 1944, p.24
[326] A.G. Kokin and others, *Tyazheliy Tank. Rukovodstvo*, Military Publisher of the People's Commissariat of Defense, Moscow, 1944, p.281
[327] A.G. Kokin and others, *Tyazheliy Tank. Rukovodstvo*, Military Publisher of the People's Commissariat of Defense, Moscow, 1944, p.279
[328] A.G. Kokin and others, *Tyazheliy Tank. Rukovodstvo*, Military Publisher of the People's Commissariat of Defense, Moscow, 1944, p.34
[329] A.G. Kokin and others, *Tyazheliy Tank. Rukovodstvo*, Military Publisher of the People's Commissariat of Defense, Moscow, 1944, p.39-40
[330] A.G. Kokin and others, *Tyazheliy Tank. Rukovodstvo*, Military Publisher of the People's Commissariat of Defense, Moscow, 1944, p.3

IS-2 tank turret roof, Nizhnekamsk. This angle shows the commander's cupola (the original hatch flaps are missing), loader's hatch and balancing torsion bar, ventilation fan cover, and the loader's MK-4 periscope. *(Nikita Trutnev)*

Rear of an IS-2 turret showing the machine gun mount on the left side, behind the commander's cupola. The machine gun mount's external mantlet is missing. *(Nikita Trutnev)*

The D-25T main gun and coaxial machine gun are installed in a gun mount attached to the front of the turret. The full length of the gun including the muzzle brake is 5840 mm. The bore axis height is 1940 mm. The nominal recoil length of the gun is 530-550 mm with a maximum recoil length of 560 mm. The gun mount offers -3 degrees of gun depression and 20 degrees of gun elevation.[331] The gun mount is equipped with a travel lock, which locks the gun at an elevation of 15 degrees. A recoil guard protects the crew during combat. During travel it can be folded down.[332]

The fighting compartment spans the center of the hull and the turret. The turret contains the loader's seat (to the right of the gun), the gunner's seat (to the left of the gun) and the commander's seat (to the left of the gun behind the gunner). The main armament (a D-25T gun and a coaxial machine gun) is housed here. A second machine gun is installed in the rear of the turret, pointing backwards. Electrical equipment installed in the turret receives power through a slip ring. Two hatches are installed in the roof, one with one flap above the loader, one with two flaps in the commander's cupola.[333] The fighting compartment is illuminated via two lights on the ceiling. Two additional lights illuminate the radio and turret ring. There is also a socket for a portable backup lamp in the electrical panel.[334]

Shells for the main gun are stored inside the turret bustle. There are two racks with 12 shells each stored vertically and two racks of two shells stored horizontally, for a total of 28 shells. Propellant casings are stored on the pannier sides (8 casings, 4 per side), on the right wall of the turret (2 casings), and on the front of the turret to the right of the gun (2

[331] A.G. Kokin and others, *Tyazheliy Tank. Rukovodstvo*, Military Publisher of the People's Commissariat of Defense, Moscow, 1944, p.408

[332] A.G. Kokin and others, *Tyazheliy Tank. Rukovodstvo*, Military Publisher of the People's Commissariat of Defense, Moscow, 1944, p.419

[333] A.G. Kokin and others, *Tyazheliy Tank. Rukovodstvo*, Military Publisher of the People's Commissariat of Defense, Moscow, 1944, pp.4-5

[334] A.G. Kokin and others, *Tyazheliy Tank. Rukovodstvo*, Military Publisher of the People's Commissariat of Defense, Moscow, 1944, p.278

casings). The majority of the casings are stored on the floor: 3 behind each fuel tank, 8 more in metallic boxes of two each. Two of the middle boxes have an extra casing carried on top. 28 casings are carried in total. 26 machine gun magazines are stored in crates in the fighting compartment, two racks of 4 magazines each are located on the front left side of the turret, and 3 magazines are carried on the right side of the turret for a total of 37 magazines.[335] On tanks with DShK machine guns, a rack for ammunition boxes is installed on the right side of the turret.[336]

5 racks for F-1 grenades are attached to the left side of the turret, 3 racks to the right side. Each rack contains two grenades. 9 more grenades are stored in bags on the left side of the turret bustle for a total of 25 grenades. There is also a flare gun stored here. Flares are stored in a box mounted on the turret ring in front of the commander's seat.[337] Some tools and spare periscope prisms are also carried in the turret bustle.[338]

Commander's Position

The commander observes through six observation slits in the commander's cupola protected with triplex tempered glass or a rotating MK-IV periscope installed in the front flap of the cupola hatch.[339] The observation slits are closed with armored shutters when not in use and framed with leather padding on the inside to protect the user from bumps. The hatch can rotate as well to make it easier for the commander

[335] A.G. Kokin and others, *Tyazheliy Tank. Rukovodstvo*, Military Publisher of the People's Commissariat of Defense, Moscow, 1944, p.423-424

[336] A.G. Solyankin and others, *Sovetskiye tyazheliye tanki 1941-1945*, Tseyghaus, Moscow, 2007, p.62

[337] A.G. Kokin and others, *Tyazheliy Tank. Rukovodstvo*, Military Publisher of the People's Commissariat of Defense, Moscow, 1944, p.40

[338] A.G. Kokin and others, *Tyazheliy Tank. Rukovodstvo*, Military Publisher of the People's Commissariat of Defense, Moscow, 1944, p.41-42

[339] A.G. Kokin and others, *Tyazheliy Tank. Rukovodstvo*, Military Publisher of the People's Commissariat of Defense, Moscow, 1944, pp.4-5

to observe. The hatch as well as its flaps can be locked in place. Springs are used to make the turret hatch easier to open.[340] The seat itself is mounted on the turret ring. It can be rotated, adjusted horizontally or vertically, be folded up or removed altogether.[341] A travel lock is located on the turret ring near the commander's seat.[342]

The commander also operates the 10-R or 10-RK radio set located behind him in the turret bustle. The radio has a voice communication range of 20-25 km in motion or 35-40 km when the tank is still. It is also capable of telegraph transmission, in which case the range is greater. The crew can communicate amongst themselves using the TPU-4-bis-F intercom device. All four crewmen have ports at their station to plug in their *shlemofon* (helmet-telephone).[343] In addition to communicating with each other, the commander and gunner can use their intercom to patch directly into the radio.[344]

---

[340] A.G. Kokin and others, *Tyazheliy Tank. Rukovodstvo*, Military Publisher of the People's Commissariat of Defense, Moscow, 1944, p.42

[341] A.G. Kokin and others, *Tyazheliy Tank. Rukovodstvo*, Military Publisher of the People's Commissariat of Defense, Moscow, 1944, p.48

[342] A.G. Kokin and others, *Tyazheliy Tank. Rukovodstvo*, Military Publisher of the People's Commissariat of Defense, Moscow, 1944, p.47

[343] A.G. Kokin and others, *Tyazheliy Tank. Rukovodstvo*, Military Publisher of the People's Commissariat of Defense, Moscow, 1944, p.25

[344] A.G. Kokin and others, *Tyazheliy Tank. Rukovodstvo*, Military Publisher of the People's Commissariat of Defense, Moscow, 1944, p.345

Commander's cupola of an IS-2 tank installed as a monument near Noviy Uchkhoz, Leningrad Oblast. The opening in the forward flap on the commander's cupola fit a MK-4 periscope. (*Nikita Trutnev*)

Gunner's Position

The gunner is positioned on the left side of the turret, in front of the commander. He is equipped with a manual and an electric turret traverse. The flywheel handle of the manual traverse also contains the electric and backup manual triggers for the coaxial machine gun.[345] Both the electric and manual traverse can be used at the same time.[346] The electric turret traverse is powered by a MB-20K motor that offers three speeds (nominally 0.8, 1.11, and 1.59 RPM respectively, these values can be greater in optimal conditions) in each direction.[347] The elevation

[345] A.G. Kokin and others, *Tyazheliy Tank. Rukovodstvo*, Military Publisher of the People's Commissariat of Defense, Moscow, 1944, p.41

[346] A.G. Kokin and others, *Tyazheliy Tank. Rukovodstvo*, Military Publisher of the People's Commissariat of Defense, Moscow, 1944, p.50

[347] A.G. Kokin and others, *Tyazheliy Tank. Rukovodstvo*, Military Publisher of the People's Commissariat of Defense, Moscow, 1944, p.306

mechanism flywheel contains the electric trigger for the main gun.[348] The gun can also be fired using the manual backup trigger installed on the left side of the recoil guard.[349] The gunner observes the battlefield and aims the gun using either the 10T-17 telescopic sight or PT4-17 periscopic sight.[350] The gunner's seat is attached to a slip ring column. The seat can rotate around the column and be adjusted horizontally. The seat can be locked in place once adjusted. The gunner's seat also has a footrest.[351] A carbon tetrachloride fire extinguisher is carried in the front left part of the turret near the gunner's station.[352]

Starting in March of 1944 IS-2 tanks were produced with TSh-17 telescopic sights and MK-4 periscopes instead of the 10T-17 and PT4-17.[353]

Loader's Position

The loader is positioned on the right side of the turret. In addition to loading the main gun, he reloads both the coaxial machine gun and fixed hull machine gun. The loader has a hatch above his head. It can lock in either the open or closed position. A torsion bar is included to make the hatch easier to open.[354] The loader's seat is identical to the gunner's

---

[348] A.G. Kokin and others, *Tyazheliy Tank. Rukovodstvo*, Military Publisher of the People's Commissariat of Defense, Moscow, 1944, p.278

[349] A.G. Kokin and others, *Tyazheliy Tank. Rukovodstvo*, Military Publisher of the People's Commissariat of Defense, Moscow, 1944, p.420

[350] A.G. Kokin and others, *Tyazheliy Tank. Rukovodstvo*, Military Publisher of the People's Commissariat of Defense, Moscow, 1944, p.407

[351] A.G. Kokin and others, *Tyazheliy Tank. Rukovodstvo*, Military Publisher of the People's Commissariat of Defense, Moscow, 1944, p.48

[352] A.G. Kokin and others, *Tyazheliy Tank. Rukovodstvo*, Military Publisher of the People's Commissariat of Defense, Moscow, 1944, p.375

[353] A.G. Solyankin and others, *Sovetskiye tyazheliye tanki 1941-1945*, Tseyghaus, Moscow, 2007, pp.59-60

[354] A.G. Kokin and others, *Tyazheliy Tank. Rukovodstvo*, Military Publisher of the People's Commissariat of Defense, Moscow, 1944, pp.43-44

seat, with the exception of the footrest.[355] A loading tray is included to assist the loader with loading the gun.[356]

The batteries are housed in the fighting compartment in frames above the fifth and sixth torsion bars.[357] They are installed perpendicular to the hull in front of the slip ring.[358]

The fighting compartment also contains the space heater and a portion of the toolkit in the hull.[359] A first aid kit, container with drinking water, and a portion of the toolkit are carried in the rear of the fighting compartment, attached to the engine bulkhead. Four hatches in the bulkhead allow access to the engine compartment without exiting the tank. Two of the hatches include observation ports covered by glass for visual inspection of the engine.[360]

Engine Compartment

The engine compartment is located behind the fighting compartment, separated from it by a bulkhead. The engine is located here, mounted on a frame. An 85 liter fuel tank is located on the right side of the engine compartment, the oil tanks are on the left. Oil radiators are located above the tanks. VT-5 Multicyclone air cleaners are installed in the front left and front right of the engine compartment.[361] They can be accessed

---

[355] A.G. Kokin and others, *Tyazheliy Tank. Rukovodstvo*, Military Publisher of the People's Commissariat of Defense, Moscow, 1944, p.48

[356] A.G. Kokin and others, *Tyazheliy Tank. Rukovodstvo*, Military Publisher of the People's Commissariat of Defense, Moscow, 1944, p.423

[357] A.G. Kokin and others, *Tyazheliy Tank. Rukovodstvo*, Military Publisher of the People's Commissariat of Defense, Moscow, 1944, p.28

[358] A.G. Kokin and others, *Tyazheliy Tank. Rukovodstvo*, Military Publisher of the People's Commissariat of Defense, Moscow, 1944, p.279

[359] A.G. Kokin and others, *Tyazheliy Tank. Rukovodstvo*, Military Publisher of the People's Commissariat of Defense, Moscow, 1944, pp.4-5

[360] A.G. Kokin and others, *Tyazheliy Tank. Rukovodstvo*, Military Publisher of the People's Commissariat of Defense, Moscow, 1944, p.37

[361] A.G. Kokin and others, *Tyazheliy Tank. Rukovodstvo*, Military Publisher of the People's Commissariat of Defense, Moscow, 1944, pp.5, 7, 19

for cleaning through maintenance hatches in the engine compartment bulkhead.[362] The V-2-IS engine is a four stroke solid injection V-12 diesel engine with an angle between cylinders equal to 60 degrees. The diameter of each cylinder is 150 mm. The total volume of all cylinders is 38.88 L. The engine weighs 1000 kg. The engine outputs up to 520 hp at 2200 RPM with a minimum speed of 500 RPM. The nominal fuel efficiency is 170-185 grams of fuel per horsepower per hour and no more than 15 grams of oil per horsepower per hour.[363] The engine can either be started with the inertial-electric starter or the compressed air starter.[364] In addition to the main engine, the engine compartment contains an electric generator.[365] Two lights located underneath the engine illuminate this compartment.[366] The tank carries a total of 520 liters of diesel fuel in internal tanks and additional fuel in external tanks (100 liters each).[367]

The Rear

The rear of the tank is composed of three separate plates. The lower plate is welded to the floor of the tank and the vertical sides. Two tow hooks with sprung clips are located here as well as holders for two spare track links. Hinges of the middle rear plate are welded to the top of the lower rear plate. The middle rear plate is mounted to the top of these hinges and also held on with 12 bolts. A torsion bar is included to make it easier to open the rear middle plate for transmission maintenance.

---

[362] A.G. Kokin and others, *Tyazheliy Tank. Rukovodstvo*, Military Publisher of the People's Commissariat of Defense, Moscow, 1944, p.133

[363] A.G. Kokin and others, *Tyazheliy Tank. Rukovodstvo*, Military Publisher of the People's Commissariat of Defense, Moscow, 1944, pp.4-5

[364] A.G. Kokin and others, *Tyazheliy Tank. Rukovodstvo*, Military Publisher of the People's Commissariat of Defense, Moscow, 1944, p.359

[365] A.G. Kokin and others, *Tyazheliy Tank. Rukovodstvo*, Military Publisher of the People's Commissariat of Defense, Moscow, 1944, p.278

[366] A.G. Kokin and others, *Tyazheliy Tank. Rukovodstvo*, Military Publisher of the People's Commissariat of Defense, Moscow, 1944, p.278

[367] A.G. Kokin and others, *Tyazheliy Tank. Rukovodstvo*, Military Publisher of the People's Commissariat of Defense, Moscow, 1944, p.19

There are two inspection ports 496 mm in diameter in the middle rear plate. The upper rear plate is attached to brackets welded to the sloped superstructure sides with 16 bolts and can also be removed to make maintenance easier. Tow hook carriers are affixed to the upper rear plate.[368] On tanks produced after September 1st, 1944, two hinges for a barrel clamp are attached to the upper rear place.[369]

Rear of an IS-2M tank, Kubinka Tank Museum. The barrel clamp was added in September of 1944. *(Nikita Trutnev)*

The Engine Deck

The engine deck is attached with 20 bolts to brackets welded to the sloped superstructure sides as well as a beam that runs across between the transmission and engine compartments. The engine deck can be

---

[368] A.G. Kokin and others, *Tyazheliy Tank. Rukovodstvo*, Military Publisher of the People's Commissariat of Defense, Moscow, 1944, pp.34-35
[369] A.G. Solyankin and others, *Sovetskiye tyazheliye tanki 1941-1945*, Tseyghaus, Moscow, 2007, p.60

removed for maintenance. A hatch for access to the engine without removing the engine deck is also included. An opening for refilling engine coolant exists at the center of the hatch. The transmission compartment deck consists of two grates made out of angle bars. A series of shutters that can be adjusted using knobs on the engine compartment bulkhead control how much air can enter the transmission compartment through these grates. The transmission compartment deck is attached to the beam that runs between the engine compartment and transmission compartment as well as the upper rear plate and sides with 12 bolts. Like the engine deck, it can be removed for maintenance.[370] Two convoy lights are mounted on top of the transmission compartment, one on each side.[371]

The transmission compartment is located in the rear of the tank, separated from the engine compartment by a bulkhead. The transmission compartment houses the main clutch, the cooling fan, the gearbox, planetary turning mechanisms, and final drives. The water radiators are located on the bulkhead between the engine and transmission compartment, underneath the cooling fan. The gearbox, clutch, and turning mechanisms are operated by the driver using control rods that run along the floor of the fighting and engine compartments.[372] The main clutch is a multi-disk dry friction type with a semi-rigid linkage to the gearbox. The gearbox offers 8 forward and 2 reverse gears.[373] A servo mechanism is installed in the transmission compartment to make the clutch easier to operate.[374] The transmission

---

[370] A.G. Kokin and others, *Tyazheliy Tank. Rukovodstvo*, Military Publisher of the People's Commissariat of Defense, Moscow, 1944, pp.35-36
[371] A.G. Kokin and others, *Tyazheliy Tank. Rukovodstvo*, Military Publisher of the People's Commissariat of Defense, Moscow, 1944, p.279
[372] A.G. Kokin and others, *Tyazheliy Tank. Rukovodstvo*, Military Publisher of the People's Commissariat of Defense, Moscow, 1944, pp.16-17
[373] A.G. Kokin and others, *Tyazheliy Tank. Rukovodstvo*, Military Publisher of the People's Commissariat of Defense, Moscow, 1944, p.21
[374] A.G. Kokin and others, *Tyazheliy Tank. Rukovodstvo*, Military Publisher of the People's Commissariat of Defense, Moscow, 1944, p.193

compartment is illuminated with two lights, one on each side. There is also a socket for a portable backup lamp on the left side.[375]

Engine deck of the IS-2M tank, Kubinka Tank Museum. The engine and transmission compartment air intakes can be seen, as well as the exhaust manifold. The rear machine gun was replaced by an extra ventilation fan as a part of the IS-2M modernization process. (*Nikita Trutnev*)

Each final drive powers a drive sprocket located in the rear of the hull. Each drive sprocket has two removable crowns with 14 teeth apiece. The drive sprocket weighs 356 kg.[376] The sprockets engage with a track composed of 86 links (43 with guide horn and 43 without). The track links are joined together by track pins, which are then locked in place with a nut and a locking ring.[377] Each link is 650 mm wide. A fully assembled track weighs 2000 kg. There are two idlers in the front of the

[375] A.G. Kokin and others, *Tyazheliy Tank. Rukovodstvo*, Military Publisher of the People's Commissariat of Defense, Moscow, 1944, p.278

[376] A.G. Kokin and others, *Tyazheliy Tank. Rukovodstvo*, Military Publisher of the People's Commissariat of Defense, Moscow, 1944, p.23

[377] A.G. Kokin and others, *Tyazheliy Tank. Rukovodstvo*, Military Publisher of the People's Commissariat of Defense, Moscow, 1944, p.263

tank that are adjustable to tension the track. Each idler weighs 290 kg. The idlers are interchangeable with the road wheels. There are six road wheels and three return rollers (95 kg each) per side. Each road wheel is connected to a torsion bar with a maximum travel of 28 degrees.[378]

The track is nominally tensioned to the point where it dips 40-50 mm below the return rollers at its lowest point. If the track links are so worn out that this gap is too wide even at maximum tension, one track link without a guide horn is discarded. When driving on dirt or country roads the tracks are moderately slackened, when driving on sand, snow, or mud the tracks are slackened even more.[379]

Underside of the IS-2 tank in Nizhnekamsk showing the inner side of one road wheel with the suspension arm visible. Each suspension arm is attached to a torsion bar that is attached to the opposite side of the hull. *(Nikita Trutnev)*

[378] A.G. Kokin and others, *Tyazheliy Tank. Rukovodstvo*, Military Publisher of the People's Commissariat of Defense, Moscow, 1944, p.23, 268
[379] A.G. Kokin and others, *Tyazheliy Tank. Rukovodstvo*, Military Publisher of the People's Commissariat of Defense, Moscow, 1944, p.263-264

Profile of the IS-2 tank in Nizhnekamsk showing the running gear. The track intentionally has some slack in it to allow the road wheels to move up and down on uneven terrain without stressing the track pins. On difficult terrain such as sand, snow, or mud the tracks are slackened even more. *(Nikita Trutnev)*

Appendix 1: Glossary

ABTU: *Avto-bronetankovoye Upravleniye*, Automobile, Armored Vehicle, and Tank Directorate. Formed on November 22nd, 1934 to manage design, testing, and production of armored and unarmored vehicles for the army, as well as training in their use. Reformed into the **GABTU** (*Glavnoye Avto-bronetankovoye Upravleniye*, Main Automobile, Armored Vehicle, and Tank Directorate) on June 26th, 1940. After reorganization in December of 1942 the **GBTU** (*Glavnoye Bronetankovoye Upravleniye*, Main Armored Vehicle and Tank Directorate) was responsible only for managing tank design, testing, and production.[380]

ChTZ: *Chelyabinskiy Traktorniy Zavod*, Chelyabinsk Tractor Factory. After the evacuation of LKZ to the Urals the two factories amalgamated into **ChKZ** (*Chelyabinskiy Kirovskiy Zavod*, Kirov Factory in Chelyabinsk).

Factory #9: A factory specializing in tank and SPG gun production located in Sverdlovsk. Weapons designed at this factory had the letter D in their index (e.g., D-25).

Factory #100: A factory in Chelyabinsk spun off from ChKZ to focus on experimental development.

Factory #200: A metallurgical factory in Chelyabinsk.

GABTU: See **ABTU.**

GAU: *Glavonoye Artilleriyeskoye Upravleniye*, Main Artillery Directorate. This organization was in charge of developing all sorts of artillery, including tank guns and SPGs.

GBTU: See **ABTU.**

---

[380] RGVA F.4 Op.11 D.73 L.341-342

GKO alternatively **GOKO:** *Gosudarstvenniy Komitet Oborony,* State Committee of Defense. This was the highest ranking entity in charge of defense production and organization in 1941-1945.

GANIOP: *Gorohovetskiy Artilleriyskiy Nauchno-Issledovatelniy Opytniy Poligon,* Gorokhovets Scientific Research Experimental Artillery Proving Grounds located in the vicinity of the village of Mulino near the town of Gorokhovets.

IS: Iosif Stalin, General Secretary of the Communist Party and leader of the USSR. A series of Soviet heavy tanks produced in 1943-1953 were named after him. In Western literature the designations of these tanks are sometimes stylized as **JS**.

ISU: A portmanteau of **IS** and **SU**, a self propelled gun or howitzer motor carriage on an IS chassis.

KA: See RKKA.

Kubinka: See **NIBT Proving Grounds.**

KV: Kliment Voroshilov, a prominent Soviet military and political leader. A series of Soviet heavy tanks produced in 1939-1943 were named after him.

LKZ: *Leningradskiy Kirovskiy Zavod,* Kirov Factory in Leningrad.

NIBT Proving Grounds: *Nauchno-Issledovatelniy Bronetakoviy Poligon,* Scientific Research Armored Vehicle Proving Grounds. Located in Kubinka. Presently the site of the Kubinka Tank Museum and Patriot Park.

NKTP: *Narodniy Komissariat Tankovoy Promyshlennosti,* People's Commissariat of Tank Production. This government entity managed factories involved in tank production that were previously distributed among other People's Commissariats.

NKV: *Narodniy Komissariat Vooruzheniya,* People's Commissariat of Armament.

Object ###: An internal factory designation for experimental armored vehicles. The designation "Object" is followed by a three digit number corresponding to the blueprints number for the vehicle. The convention only entered use in 1943, and vehicles developed prior to that were usually referred to by the three digit number alone.

RKKA: *Raboche-Krestyanskaya Krasnaya Armya,* Worker and Peasant Red Army. The prefix "Worker and Peasant" was gradually phased out in the late 1930s and by the Great Patriotic War the abbreviation was reduced to KA (*Krasnaya Armiya,* Red Army).

RPM: Rounds Per Minute, a unit of measurement of the rate of fire.

SKB-2: *Spetsializirovannoye Konstruktorskoye Byuro 2,* Specialized Design Bureau #2. This design bureau at Kirov Factory was responsible for the design of heavy tanks, among other projects.

SPG: Self Propelled Gun.

ss: *sovershenno sekretno,* top secret (lit. "completely secret").

SU: *Samokhodnaya Ustanovka,* self propelled gun or howitzer carriage.

TPU: *Tankovoye Peregovornoye Ustroystvo,* Tank Intercom Device.

TsAKB: *Tsentralnoye Artilleriyskoye Konstruktorskoye Byuro,* Central Artillery Design Bureau. Weapons designed by this bureau had the letter S in their index (e.g., S-31).

UZTM: *Uralskiy Zavod Tyazhelogo Mashinostroyeniya,* Ural Heavy Machinebuilding Factory.

ZIS: *Zavod Imeni Stalina,* an automotive factory named after Stalin.

Appendix 2: D-25T Gun Data

Table 2: D-25T gun[381]

D-25T 122mm gun		
Caliber	121.920	mm
Length (with muzzle brake)	5933.000	mm
Length (rifled section only)	4359.300	mm
Rifling depth	1.015	mm
Rifling groove	6.120	mm
Rifling land	2.495	mm
Rifling count	44	
Pitch of rifling	25	calibers
Maximum recoil resistance	39	tons
Nominal recoil length	490 - 550	mm
Maximum recoil length	570.000	mm
Weight		
Complete assembly with mantlet	2880	kg
Complete assembly without mantlet	2400	kg
All recoiling elements	1970	kg
Barrel and breech only	1935	kg
Breech	65	kg

381 TsAMO RF F.38 Op.11369 D.490 L.77; *Tablitsy strelby 122-mm tankkovoy pushki obr.1943 g (D-25T) TS #144T*, Ministry of Defense of the USSR, Moscow, 1969, 7th edition

Table 3: Ammunition[382]

Propellant casing	
Mass	15.4 kg
Length	780 mm

Armor piercing shell BR-471	
Mass	25 kg
Length (less fuse)	2.9 calibers
Muzzle velocity	795 m/s
HE content	0.16 kg

Armor piercing shell with ballistic cap BR-471B	
Mass	25 kg
Length (less fuse)	3.4 calibers
Muzzle velocity	795 m/s
HE content	0.16 kg

High explosive shell OF-471N and OF-471NZh (whole body shortened type)	
Mass	25 kg
Length (less fuse)	4.5 calibers
Muzzle velocity	795 m/s
HE content	3.35 kg

---

[382] *Tablitsy strelby 122-mm tankkovoy pushki obr.1943 g (D-25T) TS #144T*, Ministry of Defense of the USSR, Moscow, 1969, 7th edition

High explosive shell OF-471N (screw-in tip type)

Mass	25 kg
Length (less fuse)	4.6 calibers
Muzzle velocity	795 m/s
HE content	3.8 kg

High explosive shell OF-471 (both whole body and screw-in tip type)

Mass	25 kg
Length (less fuse)	4.7 calibers
Muzzle velocity	795 m/s
HE content	3.6 kg

Practice shot PBR-471

Mass	25 kg
Length (less fuse)	3.4 calibers
Muzzle velocity	795 m/s
HE content	none

Table 4: Calculated limit of complete penetration (rounded to the nearest 5 mm)[383]

Range (m)	BR-471		BR-471B	
	At 30 deg	At normal	At 30 deg	At normal
500	120	150	125	155
1000	105	130	120	145
1500	95	115	110	135
2000	80	100	100	125
2500	70	90	90	115
3000	65	75	85	105

[383] *Tablitsy strelby 122-mm tankkovoy pushki obr.1943 g (D-25T) TS #144T*, Ministry of Defense of the USSR, Moscow, 1969, 7th edition

Appendix 3: Tactical & Technical Data

Table 5: Technical Data of IS series tanks

	KV-13 / IS-85		
	KV-13 (February 1942)	KV-13(June 1942)	IS-85(May 1943)
Weight (tons)	34-35	35	43-44
Armor (mm/deg)			
Hull front (upper)	85-120/-	100/-	120/-
Hull front (middle)	-	-	-
Hull front (lower)	-	-	-
Hull sides (upper)	60	80-85	90
Hull sides (lower)	60	60	-
Hull rear	60	80-85	60
Turret front	85-129	-	100
Turret sides	60	-	-
Turret rear	60	-	-
Engine power (hp)	500-600	600	600
Top speed (kph)	60	50	35-37
Armament	76 mm ZIS-5	76 mm ZIS-5	85 mm(unspecified)

IS-1

	IS-1(February 1943)	IS-1(September 1943)	IS-1(production)
Weight (tons)	37.1	43.5-44	44
Armor (mm/deg)			
Hull front (upper)	120/30	120/30	120/30
Hull front (middle)	60/72	60/72	60/72
Hull front (lower)	100/40	100/30	100/30
Hull sides (upper)	90	100	90/15
Hull sides (lower)	-	90	90/0
Hull rear	60	60	Upper: 60/49 Lower: 60/41
Turret front	100	100	100/curved
Turret sides	100	-	100/18
Turret rear	-	-	100/30
Engine power (hp)	600	Maximum: 600 Nominal: 520	520 *
Top speed (kph)	55	35-40	37.7 **
Armament	76 mm F-34	85 mm D-5T	85 mm D-5T

IS-2

	IS-2(February 1943)	IS-2(October 1943)	IS-2(early)	IS-2(late)
Weight (tons)	37.9	45.5-46	46	46
Armor (mm/deg)				
Hull front (upper)	120/30	120/30	120/30	100/60 (cast) 90/60 (rolled)
Hull front (middle)	60/72	60/72	60/72	N/A
Hull front (lower)	100/40	100/30	100/30	130/30 (cast) 90/30 (rolled)
Hull sides (upper)	90	100	90/15	90/15
Hull sides (lower)	-	90	90/0	90/0
Hull rear	60	60	Upper: 60/49 Lower: 60/41	Upper: 60/49 Lower: 60/41
Turret front	100	100	100/curved	100/curved
Turret sides	100	-	100/18	100/18
Turret rear	-	-	100/30	100/30
Engine power (hp)	600	Maximum: 600 Nominal: 520	520 *	520 *
Top speed (kph)	55	32-35	37.7 **	37.7 **
Armament	122 mm U-11	122 mm D-25T	122 mm D-25T	122 mm D-25T

A value of "-" means that this requirement was not explicitly given in the respective document.
* At 2000 RPM
** At 1800 RPM

Sources for the respective entries in the tables:
KV-13 (February 1942)[384]
KV-13 (June 1942)[385]
IS-1 (February 1943)[386]
IS-2 (February 1943)
IS-85 (May 1943)[387]
IS-1 (September 1943)[388]
IS-2 (October 1943)[389]
IS-1 (production variant)[390]
IS-2 (early)[391]
IS-2 (late)[392]

[384] Y. Pasholok, *Perviy KV Pod Neschastlivym Nomerom*, https://warspot.ru/9279-pervyy-kv-pod-neschastlivym-nomerom, retrieved on July 18th, 2021
[385] RGASPI F.644 Op.2 D.69 L.74
[386] RGASPI F.644 Op.2 D.138 L.194-195
[387] TsAMO RF F.38 Op.11355 D.1380 L.185-186
[388] RGASPI F.644 Op.2 D.211 L.10-11
[389] RGASPI F.644 Op.2 D.239 L.103
[390] A.G. Kokin and others, *Tyazheliy Tank. Rukovodstvo*, Military Publisher of the People's Commissariat of Defense, Moscow, 1944, pp.9-11
[391] A.G. Kokin and others, *Tyazheliy Tank. Rukovodstvo*, Military Publisher of the People's Commissariat of Defense, Moscow, 1944, p.408
[392] A.G. Solyankin and others, *Sovetskiye tyazheliye tanki 1941-1945*, Tseyghaus, Moscow, 2007, p.124

Appendix 4: Designations

Table 6: of Great Patriotic War Era IS Series Tanks in Chronological Order

	Blueprint number	Other names used	Notes
KV-13	233	IS-1	Prototype only
IS-2	234		Prototype only
IS-1	237	IS, IS-85, IS with 85 mm gun, IS-3	Produced from October 1943 to January 1944
IS-2	240	IS-122, IS with 122 mm gun, KV-122	Produced from December 1943 to June 1945
IS-4	245		Prototype only, IS-1 tank with a 100 mm D-10T gun.
IS-5	248		Prototype only, IS-2 tank with a 100 mm S-34 gun
IS-4	701		Produced from 1946 to 1949
IS-6	252, 253		Prototype only
IS-3	703		Produced from March 1945 to July 1946

Bibliography

Primary sources

Archives

RGASPI: *Rossiyskiy Gosudarstvennyi Arkhiv Sotsialno-Politicheskoy Istorii,* Russian State Archive of Sociopolitical History

RGVA: *Rossiyskiy Gosudarstvennyi Voyenny Arkhiv,* Russian State Military Archive

RGAE: *Rossiyskiy Gosudarstvenniy Arkhiv Economiki,* Russian State Economics Archive

GA RF: *Gosudarstvennyy Arkhiv Rossiyskoy Federatsii,* State Archive of the Russian Federation

TsAMO RF: *Tsentral'nyy Arkhiv Ministerstva Oborony Rossiyskoy Federatsii,* Central Archive of the Ministry of Defense of the Russian Federation

GA RF F.R-8418 Op.28 D.2 L.72-79 *Postanovleniye STO SSSR #71ss/o "O sisteme tankovogo vooruzheniya RKKA"*

RGAE F.2097 Op.1 D.1077 L.19 (reverse)-20 *Protokol #17447ss zasedaniya podkommissii zamestitelya predsedatelya VSNKh SSSR N. Osinskogo o vypolnenii promyshlenostyu programmy vooruzheniya NKVM SSSR po sisteme tanko-traktornogo vooruzheniya*

RGAE F.7297 Op.38 D.32 L.10 *Raport Glavonogo voyenno-mobilizatsinnogo upravleniya NKTP SSSR narkomu tyazholoy*

117

promyshlennosti SSSR S. Ordzhonikidze o hode realizatsii sistemy tankovogo vooruzheniya RKKA

RGAE F.8752 Op.7 D.11 L.13 *Bronya vysokoy tversosti dlya tyazhelikh tankov IS*

RGAE F.8752 Op.4 D.303 L.121 *Order of the People's Commissar of Tank Production #425ss dated July 23rd, 1943*

RGASPI F.17 Op.162 D.8 L.18-19 *Postanovleniye politbyuro TsK VKP(b) "O vypolnenii tanko-traktornoy programmy"*

RGASPI F.644 Op.1 D.22 L.6 *Dokument 1331ss. Ob umenshenii vesa tankov KV-1*

RGASPI F.644 Op.1 D.38 L.260-263 *Dokument 1878s Ob uluchshenii tankov KV-1*

RGASPI F.644 Op.1 D.182 L.248 *Dokument 4767ss O plane proizvodstva tanrkov, samokhodnykh ustanovok, dizeley, zapasnykh chastey, i remonta tankov, samokhodnykh ustanovok, i dizeley na dekabr 1943 g*

RGASPI F.644 Op.1 D.317 L.1-159 *Dokument 6706ss O plane proizvodstva tankov, samohodnyh artillerijskih ustanovok, dizelej, zapasnyh chastej k nim i remonte tankov, artsamohodov i dizelej na 4 kvartal 1944 g.*

RGASPI F.644 Op.1 D.323 L.42-44 *Dokument 6723s Ob ustanovke krupnokalibernykh zenitnykh pulemyotov DShK na samokhodnykh artilleriyskikh ustanovkah i tankakh IS*

RGASPI F.644 Op.1 D.330 L.113-118 *Dokument 6868s Ob uluchshenii jekspluatacii tankov, samohodnyh artillerijskih ustanovok i o povyshenii kachestva ih izgotovlenija.*

RGASPI F.644 Op.2 D.138 L.194-197 Dokument 2943ss. *Ob izgotovlenii opytnykh obraztsov tankov IS*

RGASPI F.644 Op.2 D.156 L.92-95 Dokument 3290ss. *O vosstanovlenii proizvodstva 122-mm korpusnyh pushek obrazca 1931-1937 g. i izgotovlenii opytnyh obrazcov legkih korpusnyh pushek.*

RGASPI F.644 Op.2 D.202 L.135-138 *Dokument 3891ss O proizvodstve tankov KV c 85-mm pushkoy (KV-85)*

RGASPI F.644 Op.2 D.202 L.139-148 *Dokument 3892ss Ob organizatsii proizvodstva 85-mm samokhodnykh artustanovok na baze tanka T-34 na Uralmashzavode*

RGASPI F.644 Op.2 D.21 L.80 *Dokument 735ss O formirovanii polkov PTO*

RGASPI F.644 Op.2 D.211 L.1-24 Dokument 4043ss *O proizvodstve tankov IS*

RGASPI F.644 Op.2 D.239 L.101 Dokument 4479ss *O tyazhelom tanke IS-2 so 122-mm pushkoy*

RGASPI F.644 Op.2 D.254 L.127-128 *Dokument 4850ss Ob uvelichenii proizvodstva tyazhelykh tankov, artilleriyskikh samokhodnykh ustanovok, tipa IS, i ob obespechenii ikh artilleriyskim vooruzheniyem*

RGASPI F.644 Op.2 D.254 L.177-181 *Dokument 4851ss O proektirovanii, izgotovlenii i ispytanijah opytnyh obrazcov artillerijskih orudij dlja tankov i artillerijskih samohodnyh ustanovok.*

RGASPI F.644 Op.2 D.295 L.32-41 *Dokument 5378ss Ob uvelichenii proizvodstva tyazhelikh tankov, artilleriyskikh samokhodnykh ustanovok IS, mochnykh tyazhelykh pushek i 122-152 mm snaryadov*

RGASPI F.644 Op.2 D.305 L.144-148 *Dokument 5583s Ob izgotovlenii opytnykh obraztsov novogo tyazhelogo tanka na Kirovskom zavode Narkomata tankovoy promyshlennosti*

RGASPI F.644 Op.2 D.320 L.110 *Dokument 5690s. Ob usilenii bronirovaniya bashni T-34-85*

RGASPI F.644 Op.2 D.395 L.1-2 *Dokument 6679s Ob ustanovke na tankah i artsamohodah IS dizelej V-11 moshhnost'ju 520 l.s.*

RGASPI F.644 Op.2 D.464 L.82-97 *Dokument 7950ss O modernizacii tjazhelogo tanka IS-2.*

RGASPI F.644 Op.2 D.69 L.71-76 *Dokument 1878s Ob uluchshenii tankov KV-1*

RGASPI F.644 Op.1 D.292 L.47 *Dokument 6345ss O plane proizvodstva i remonta tankov, samokhodnykh artilleriyskikh ustanovok, dizeley, i proizvodstva zapasnykh chastey k nim za avgust 1944 g*

RGASPI F.644 Op.1 D.313 L.131 *Dokument 6679s Ob ustanovke na takhah i artsamokhodah IS dizeley V-11 moschnostyu 520 l.s.*

RGASPI F.644 Op.1 D.350 L.27 *Dokument 7332ss O plane proizvodstva i remonta tankov, samokhodnykh artilleriyskikh ustanovok, dizeley i postavki tankovykh zapasnykh chastey k nim na 1 kvartal 1945 g*

RGVA F.31811 Op.1 D.38 L.2-3 *Sluzhebnaya zapiska nachalnika shtaba RKKA B.M. Shaposhnikova narkomu po voyennym i morskim delam SSSR predsedatelyu Revvoyensoveta SSSR K.Ye. Voroshilovu o zakupke obraztsov tankov za granitsey*

RGVA F.4 Op.11 D.73 L.341-342 *Prikaz Narodnogo Kommissara Oborony #0954 o reorganizatsii Glavonogo avtobronetankovogo upravleniya Krasnoy Armii*

RGVA F.4 Op.12 D.106 L.112-122 *Prikaz Narodnogo Kommissara Oborony #325 o boyevom primenenii tankovykh i mekhanizirovannykh chastey*

RGVA F.4 Op.14 D.414 L.20-22 *Protokol soveschaniya Revvoyensoveta SSSR ob izmemeniyah v tankovoy programme 1931*

RGVA F.4 Op.19 D.55 L.1-9 *Letter from Chief of the ABTU, Komkor Pavlov and Military Commissar of the ABTU Brigadier Engineer Alliluyev to Marshal of the Soviet Union Voroshilov, #3, February 21st, 1938*

RGVA F.4 Op.19 D.55 L.24-27 *Proposal of ABTU Chief D.G. Pavlov and ABTU Military Commissar P.S. Alliluyev to utilize old out of production tanks in the RKKA*

TsAMO RF F.3409 Op.1 D.6 L.200-201 *Memo from the Commander of Armored and Mechanized Forces of the Red Army #511127-s, July 19th, 1944*

TsAMO RF F.38 Op.11355 D.41 L.10-11 *Letter #SO6913 from Chief Engineer of factory #183 Makhonin and Head of Design Bureau #520 Kucherenko to GABTU KA District Engineer Kozyrev dated December 20th, 1940*

TsAMO RF F.38 Op.11355 D.697 L.27 *Zaklucheniye to proyektu ustanovki 85 mm pushki v tank "KV"*

TsAMO RF F.38 Op.11355 D.895 L.1-24 *Doklad glavnomu voyennomu sovetu krasnoy armii o novyh sredstvah borby v sovremennoy voyne po avtotankovomu i protivotankovomu vooruzheniyu*

TsAMO RF F.38 Op.11355 D.934 L.1-5 *Istoriya razvitiya tanka "KV"*

TsAMO RF F.38 Op.11355 D.935 L.184-186 *Report from Chief of the GABTU BTU Korobkov, Acting Military Commissar of the GABTU BTU Kovalev, and Chief of the 5th Department of the GABTU BTU Afonin to the Deputy People's Commissar of Defense Fedorenko dated June 1st, 1942*

TsAMO RF F.38 Op.11355 D.958 L.8 *Transcript of a phone call between Stalin and Zaltsmann, January 24th, 1942*

TsAMO RF F.38 Op.11355 D.958 L.109-110 *Letter from GABTU Military Representative Engineer-Major Fedoseyev to Chief of the 6th Department of the GABTU Armored Vehicle Directorate, #506s, September 30th, 1942*

TsAMO RF F.38 Op.11355 D.1377 L.195 *Report on experimental factory #100 projects for June 1943*

TsAMO RF F.38 Op.11355 D.1380 L.185-186 *Taktiko-tekhnicheskaya kharakteristika tanka IS*

TsAMO RF F. 38 Op.11355 D.1401 L.18-21 *Letter from Chief Engineer of the Kirov Factory Makhonin, Chief Designer of the Kirov Factory Kotin, and Chairman of the State Trials Commission Lantsberg to People's Commissar of Tank Production Zaltsman*

TsAMO RF F.38 Op.11355 D.1525 L.37-39 *Usloviya boyevogo obsluzhivaniya*

TsAMO RF F.38 Op.11355 D.1529 L.3 *Table of characteristics of 85 mm guns*

TsAMO RF F.38 Op.11355 D.1529 L.13-15 *Conclusions on trials of D-5T and S-31 guns at the Gorohovets ANIOP, August 28th, 1943*

TsAMO RF F.38 Op.11355 D.1634 L.7-8 *Excerpt from IS-1 tank trials*

TsAMO RF F.38 Op.11355 D.1660 L.12 *Letter from Lieutenant Generals of the Tank Forces Korobkov and Biryukov to the Deputy Chairman of the Committee of Defense Molotov dated April 13th, 1943*

TsAMO RF F.38 Op.11355 D.1702 L.3 *Characteristics of the D-25T tank gun*

TsAMO RF F.38 Op.11355 D.2243 L.158 *Zaklucheniye po chertezham uzlov modernizirovannogo tanka IS*

TsAMO RF F.38 Op.11355 D.2245 L.240-241 *Letter from Chief Engineer at factory #200 Nitsenko to Deputy People's Commissar of Tank Production Zernov, #1262s, June 22nd, 1944*

TsAMO RF F.38 Op.11355 D.2349 L.22 *Diagram of D-25 gunnery trial results*

TsAMO RF F.38 Op.11355 D.2369 L.24-26 *Meropriyatiya povyshayushiye boyevye kachestva tanka IS-122*

TsAMO RF F.38 Op.11355 D.2375 L.1-17 *Otchet po ispytaniyam na broneprobivayemost i skorostrelnost tankovykh pushek D-10 i D-25*

TsAMO RF F.38 Op.11355 D.2380 L.8 *Graficheskoye izobrazheniye rezultatov otstrela to opredeleniyu kuchnosti boya pushki D-25*

TsAMO RF F.38 Op.11355 D.2571 L.60 *Izvescheniye #35 ob otpravke produktsii s Kirovskogo zavoda*

TsAMO RF F.38 Op.11355 D.2852 L.15 *Diagram of D-25 gunnery trial results*

TsAMO RF F.38 Op.11355 D.2855 L.27-28 *Diagrams of D-25 gunnery trial results*

TsAMO RF F.38 Op.11355. D.2872 15-17 *Rezultaty ispytaniy, snaryadostoykost korpusov*

TsAMO RF F.38 Op.11355 D.2860 L.1-53 *Otchet po kratkim ispytaniyam nemetskogo tanka "Tigr B"*

TsAMO RF F.38 Op.11355 D.3012 L.102-105 *Report on Object 701 trials by Engineer-Colonel Blagonravov dated February 8th, 1945*

TsAMO RF F.38 Op.11369 D.1 L.70-75 *Po artsamakhodam ISU-122 i ISU-122S*

TsAMO RF F.38 Op.11369 D.28 L.1-41 *Zaklucheniye kommissii po ispytaniyu 100 mm tankovykh pushek D-10-T i S-34-T ustanovlennykh v tankakh IS*

TsAMO RF F.38 Op.11369 D.107 L.7-8 *Samokhodnaya artilleriyskaya ustanovka SU-85 po proyektu zavoda #9 NKV*

TsAMO RF F.38 Op.11369 D.490 L.4-5 *Letter from the People's Commissar of Tank Production V. Malyshev to Chief of the GAU N.D. Yakovlev, Commander of the Armored and Mechanized Forces Ya.N. Fedorenko, and People's Commissar of Armaments D.F. Ustinov dated February 9th, 1944*

TsAMO RF F.38 Op.11369 D.490 L.35-38 *Ob ustanovke v tank IS 100 mm pushki D-10 zavoda #9 NKV vmesto 122 mm pushki togo zhe zavoda*

TsAMO RF F.38 Op.11369 D.696 L.46-47 *Zaklucheniye o vozmozhnosti primeneniya unitarnogo patrona k 122mm pushkam D-25 v tankakh IS-122 i samokhodnykh artustanovkakh ISU-122S*

TsAMO RF F.38 Op.11369 D.696 L.189-193 *Kharakteristiki opytnykh obraztsov tankovykh i samokhodnykh pushek Krasnoy Armii*

TsAMO RF F.38 Op.11377 D.12 L.1-61 *Otchet po ispytaniyam bronevoy zaschity nemetskogo tanka T-VI obstrelom*

TsAMO RF F.38 Op.11377 D.129 L.1-50 *Otchet to ispytaniyu snaryadnym obstrelom lobovykh detaley korpusa i bashni nemetskogo tyazhelogo tanka "Tigr B"*

TsAMO RF F.81 Op.12104 D.201 L.11-12 *Letter from the GAU UVKA Chief Military Engineer 1st Class Lipin to the director of the Kirov Factory in Leningrad dated March 13th, 1941*

TsAMO RF F.38 Op.12104 D.261 L.7-12 *Letter from Gorohovets ANIOP Chief Colonel Sorokin to Deputy People's Commissar of Defense Marshal Kulik, #004587, July 18th, 1941*

TsAMO RF F.81 Op.12063 D.19 L.15-16 *Letter from Engineer-Major Solomonov to Colonel Zhevanik #10633, June 7th, 1943*

TsAMO RF F.81 Op.12038 D.188 L.84 *Letter from GAU Regional Engineer Engineer-Colonel Abramov to Deputy Chairman of the GAU Artillery Committee, Major General Zhevanik, #1863s, November 31st, 1943*

TsAMO RF F.81 Op.12038 D.313 L.106 *Letter from GAU Regional Engineer Engineer-Colonel Abramov to Deputy Chairman of the GAU Artillery Committee, Major General Zhevanik, #1610s, October 13th, 1943*

TsAMO RF F.81 Op.12038 D.577 L.28-31 *Proposals of new coaxial machine guns for IS-2 tanks*

TsAMO RF F.81 Op.12063 D.19 L.155-156 *Letter from Assistant Chief of Department #16 of the GAU Artillery Committee Engineer-Major Solomonov to Chief of Department #16 of the GAU Artillery Committee Colonel Zhevanik, May 31st, 1943*

TsAMO RF F.307 Op.4148 D.1 L.77-103 *Zhurnal boyevykh deystviy 2 TA s 20.12.43 po 23.2.44*

TsAMO RF F.307 Op.4148 D.189 L.107 *Letter from Marshal Fedorenko to Marshal Konev dated April 1st, 1944*

Canadian Military Headquarters, London (CMHQ), Files Block No. 55 – reel 5776, image 2713

Publications

A.G. Kokin, K.Ya. Lvovskiy, A.G. Rovinskiy, V.A. Shmelev, Ya.D. Nefedov, A.V. Pavlov, S.I. Yushin, K.N. Nikolayev, A.G. Shevyakov, A.P. Poklonov, A.M. Smirnov, G.S. Pilyavskiy, V.I. Irodov, S.G. Isayev, *Tyazheliy Tank. Rukovodstvo*, Military Publisher of the People's Commissariat of Defense, Moscow, 1944

Tablitsy strelby 122-mm tankkovoy pushki obr.1943 g (D-25T) TS #144T, Ministry of Defense of the USSR, Moscow, 1969, 7th edition

Tablitsy strelby 122-mm gaubitsy obr. 1938 g., 5th annotated edition, Military Publisher of the People's Commissariat of Defense, Moscow, 1943

Kratkiye tablitsy strelby 76-mm pushki obr. 1941 g. (ZIS-3), Military Publisher of the People's Commissariat of Defense, Moscow, 1942

Secondary sources

Books

Ye. Belash, *Tanki Mezhvoyennogo Perioda*, Tactical Press, Moscow, 2014

L Samuelson, *Plans for Stalin's War Machine*, Houndmills, Basingstoke, Hampshire and London, Macmillan Press LTD, 1999.

M.R. Habeck, *Storm of Steel The Development of Armor Doctrine in Germany and the Soviet Union, 1919–1939*, Cornell University Press, 2014, Kindle edition

A.G. Solyankin, M.V. Pavlov, I.V. Pavlov, I.G. Zheltov, *Sovietskiye Tyazheliye Tanki 1917-1941*, Tseyghaus, Moscow, 2006

A.G. Solyankin, M.V. Pavlov, I.V. Pavlov, I.G. Zheltov, Sovetskiye Sredniye Tanki 1924-1941, Tseyghaus, Moscow, 2007

A.G. Solyankin, M.V. Pavlov, I.V. Pavlov, I.G. Zheltov, *Sovetskiye Legkie Tanki 1917-1941*, Tseyghaus, Moscow, 2007

A.G. Solyankin, M.V. Pavlov, I.V. Pavlov, I.G. Zheltov, *Sovietskiye Tyazheliye Samokhodniye Artilleriyskiye Ustanovki 1941-1945*, Tseyghaus, Moscow, 2006

M. Kolomiyets, *Leningradskiye KV*, Tactical Press, Moscow, 2013

N.S. Popov, M.V. Ashik, I.V. Bakh, V.A. Dobryakov, L.M. Dmitriyeva, O.K. Ilyin, V.I. Petrov, *Konstruktor Boyevykh Mashin*, Lenizdat, Leningrad, 1988

M. Kolomiyets, *Tyazheliy Tank KV-1 Perviye Tanki Pobedy*, Eksmo, Moscow, 2017

A.M. Radionov, R.V. Mazurkevich, N.I. Lebedev, R.A. Lanikhin, D.Yu. Chebotarev, *Glavnoye Bronetankovoye Upravleniye: lyudi, sobytia, fakty v dokumentakh 1943-1944 gg kniga III*, Ministry of Defense of the Russian Federation, Moscow, 2006

Vestnik Bronetankovoy Promyshlennosti #5-6, Mintransmash, Moscow, 1946

A.M. Radionov, I.A. Groshev, N.I. Lebedev, V.I Kravchinskiy, A.V. Tikhonov, *Glavnoye Avtobronetankovoye Upravleniye Lyudi, Sobytiya, Fakty v Dokumentakh 1944-1945 kniga IV*, Moscow, 2007

M. Baryatinskiy, *Tyazheliy tank IS-2*, Yauza, Moscow, 2006

A.G. Solyankin, M.V. Pavlov, I.V. Pavlov, I.G. Zheltov, *Sovetskiye tyazheliye tanki 1941-1945*, Tseyghaus, Moscow, 2007

A. Mernikov, *Vooruzhenniye Sily SSSR i Germanii 1939-1945*, Harvest, Minsk, 2010

128

P. Ware, *M4 Sherman Tank 1941 Onwards All Variants*, Zenith Press, 2012

T. Anderson, *Panzer* IV, Osprey Publishing, 2021

N.N. Nikiforov, P.I. Turkin, A.A. Zherebtsov, S.G. Galienko, *Artilleriya*, 5th edition, Military Publisher of the Ministry of Defense, Moscow, 1953

W. Schneider, Tigers in Combat I, Stackpole Books, Mechanicsburg, 2004

A. Ulanov, D. Shein, *Perviye Tridtsatchetverki*, Tactical Press, Moscow, 2014

P. Samsonov, *Designing the T-34*, Gallantry Books, Horncastle, 2019

S. Shumilin, N. Okolelov, A. Chechin, *Sredniy Tank T-55 (object 155)*, ZAO Redaktsiya Zhurnala Modelist-Konstruktor, Moscow, 2008

R.P. Hunnicutt, *Stuart A History of the American Light Tank Volume 1, Presidio Press*, 1992.

Y. Bakhurin, *Panzerjager Tiger (P) Ferdinand*, Tactical Press, Moscow, 2014

M. Postnikov, *Bronezaschita Tyazhelikh Tankov KV i IS 1941-1945*, Eksprint, Moscow, 2006, p. 28-29

Websites

M.N. Svirin, *Bronya Krepka: Istoriya sovetskogo tanka 1917-1939*, http://militera.lib.ru/tw/svirin_mn1/03.html, retrieved on August 21st, 2021

Y. Pasholok, *Ne Poletevshiy Kak Lastochka*, *https://zen.yandex.ru/media/yuripasholok/ne-poletevshii-kak-lastochka-60114787a3e47e7ee8bf5db4* retrieved on May 9th, 2021

Y. Pasholok, *Vremennoye Usilieniye*, https://warspot.ru/12390-vremennoe-usilenie, retrieved on December 23rd, 2021

I. Afonin, *Svodka Tankovogo upravleniya Glavnogo bronetankovogo upravleniya "O nalichii tankov v Krasnoj Armii za period s 1 yanvarya 1941 goda po 1 yanvarya 1944 goda"*, *https://dentankista2018.mil.ru/*, retrieved on December 23rd, 2021

Y. Pasholok, *Perviy KV Pod Neschastlivym Nomerom*, *https://warspot.ru/9279-pervyy-kv-pod-neschastlivym-nomerom*, retrieved on May 10th, 2021

Y. Pasholok, *Predposledniy Shag*, https://warspot.ru/9483-predposledniy-shag, retrieved on May 12th, 2021

Y. Pasholok, *Gaubichniy KV*, https://warspot.ru/9026-gaubichnyy-kv, retrieved on May 15th, 2021

Y. Pasholok, *Pervoye Prishestviye IS-1*, https://warspot.ru/9911-pervoe-prishestvie-is-2, retrieved on May 15th. 2021

Y. Pasholok, *Strashnee Koshki Zverya Net*, https://warspot.ru/11907-strashnee-koshki-zverya-net, retrieved on December 15th, 2021

Y. Pasholok, *Sovetskiye Istrebiteli Tankov s Krugovym Obstrelom*, https://warspot.ru/4819-u-20-sovetskie-istrebiteli-tankov-s-krugovym-obstrelom, retrieved on May 5th, 2021

Y. Pasholok, *Opytniy Tank s Boyevoy Biografiyey*, https://warspot.ru/4884-opytnyy-tank-s-boevoy-biografiey, retrieved on May 15th, 2021

Y. Pasholok, *Bolshaya Pushka dlya Nebolshoy Bashni*, https://warspot.ru/8778-bolshaya-pushka-dlya-nebolshoy-bashni, retrieved on May 15th, 2021

Y. Pasholok, *Ot Srednego Shturmovika k Srednemu Istrebitelyu*, https://warspot.ru/10662-put-ot-srednego-shturmovika-k-srednemu-istrebitelyu, retrieved on May 16th, 2021

Y. Pasholok, *IS Kotoriy Poluchilsya*, https://warspot.ru/10487-is-kotoryy-poluchilsya, retrieved on May 16th, 2021

Y. Pasholok, *Kutsak Kotina*, https://warspot.ru/10800-kutsak-kotina, retrieved on May 16th, 2021

Y. Pasholok, *Promezhutochniy IS*, https://warspot.ru/11074-promezhutochnyy-is, retrieved on May 22nd, 2021

Y. Pasholok, *IS s Tyazhelym Vooruzheniyev*, https://warspot.ru/11233-is-s-tyazhyolym-vooruzheniem , retrieved on May 22nd, 2021

Y. Pasholok, *Tyazheliy trofey s Kurskoy dugi*, https://warspot.ru/10672-tyazhyolyy-trofey-s-kurskoy-dugi, retrieved on May 24th, 2021

Y. Pasholok, *Posledniy sovetskiy tyazheloves*, https://warspot.ru/4474-posledniy-sovetskiy-tyazheloves, retrieved on May 24th, 2021

Y. Pasholok, *Borba za mesto na konveyere*, https://warspot.ru/11457-borba-za-mesto-na-konveyere, retrieved on May 27th, 2021

Y. Pasholok, *Malaya modernizatsiya bolshogo tanka*, https://warspot.ru/12831-malaya-modernizatsiya-bolshogo-tanka, retrieved on May 30th, 2021

Y. Pasholok, *Ne popavshiy v amplitudu*, https://warspot.ru/15654-ne-popavshiy-v-amplitudu, retrieved on June 6th, 2021

Y. Pasholok, *Modernizatsia na bumage*, https://warspot.ru/12111-modernizatsiya-na-bumage, retrieved on June 6th, 2021

Y. Pasholok, *Morda klinom dlya tyazhelogo tanka*, https://zen.yandex.ru/media/yuripasholok/morda-klinom-dlia-tiajelogo-tanka-5f7eb0a715099c198a02f2f6, retrieved on June 6th, 2021

Y. Pasholok, *Slishkom dlinniy unitar*, https://zen.yandex.ru/media/yuripasholok/slishkom-dlinnyi-unitar-5fba3e769d2ffe38ee7d8cda, retrieved on June 6th, 2021.

Y. Pasholok, *Optimalnaya modernizatsiya*, https://warspot.ru/13911-optimalnaya-modernizatsiya, retrieved on June 6th, 2021

Y. Pasholok, *KV ne hochet uhodit*, https://warspot.ru/11571-kv-ne-hochet-uhodit, retrieved on June 6th, 2021

Y. Pasholok, *Na puti k samomu massovomu amerikanskomu tanku*, https://warspot.ru/17313-na-puti-k-samomu-massovomu-amerikanskomu-tanku, retrieved on February 16th, 2022

N. Barinov, *Pochemu podschet tankov malo govorit o moschi armii* https://zen.yandex.ru/media/id/5ba87f4e1c5a9600aa6b87d6/pochemu-podschet-tankov-malo-govorit-o-mosci-armii--5bc6415fcf1f9400abd53549, retrieved on July 17th, 2022

Andrey Tarasenko, *Poligonniye ispytaniya vtorogo opytnogo obraztsa tanka T-44 konstruktsii zavoda #183 NKTP*, http://btvt.info/1inservice/t-44-1944-tests.htm, retrieved on July 21st, 2022

Y. Pasholok, *Zhelezniy kaput*, https://warspot.ru/11521-zheleznyy-kaput, retrieved on July 29th, 2022

Y. Pasholok, *Krupniy kalibr dlya krupnykh KV*, https://zen.yandex.ru/media/yuripasholok/krupnyi-kalibr-dlia-krupnyh-kv-5ff34325af142f0b17d2cf6c, retrieved on August 17th, 2022

Y. Pasholok, *IS-2 Argument Kalibrom 122 mm*, https://warspot.ru/4016-is-2-argument-kalibrom-122-mm, retrieved on August 26th, 2022

Y. Pasholok, *Shag v nuzhnom napravlenii*, https://warspot.ru/14932-shag-v-nuzhnom-napravlenii, retrieved on September 28th, 2022

Y. Pasholok, *Dolgoigrayushiy IS*, https://warspot.ru/17113-dolgoigrayuschiy-is, retrieved on September 26th, 2022

Y. Pasholok, Peremennaya bronetankovaya terminologiya, https://dzen.ru/a/YGCuw9h6cDO8KQyZ?&, retrieved on September 27th, 2022

Made in the USA
Columbia, SC
24 February 2023

12949900R00074